JANE AUSTEN

Pat Levy

GREENWICH EXCHANGE
LONDON

Greenwich Exchange, London

Jane Austen

© Pat Levy, 2008

First published in Great Britain in 2008
Reprinted 2010

All rights reserved

This book is sold subject to the conditions that it shall not, by way of trade or otherwise, be lent, resold, hired out or otherwise circulated without the publisher's prior consent in any form of binding or cover other than that in which it is published and without a similiar condition including this condition being imposed on the subsequent purchaser.

Printed and bound by imprintdigital.net
Typesetting and design by Albion Associates
Cover design by December Publications
Tel: 028 90286559
Cover image: Jane Austen from a sketch by her sister Cassandra
© Mary Evans Picture Library

Greenwich Exchange Website: www.greenex.co.uk

Cataloguing in Publication Data is available
from the British Library

ISBN: 978-1-871551-89-1

Contents

Introduction		vii
1	*Northanger Abbey*	1
2	*Sense and Sensibility*	11
3	*Pride and Prejudice*	19
4	*Mansfield Park*	34
5	*Emma*	49
6	*Persuasion*	66
7	Last Words *Sanditon*	84
Bibliography		95

Introduction

It is not unusual for people to think that Jane Austen's novels are about young women finding suitable husbands. Indeed, the structure of many of Austen's novels does not seem to be altogether dissimilar from those of the classic Mills and Boon story. A young girl in difficult circumstances meets a young man with whom she falls in love, often unbeknown to herself, but falls out with him and/or encounters difficult circumstances. She meets another, duplicitous, young man but in the end comes to recognise and finally submit to her true feelings. End of story. The novels of Austen, though, concern themselves with much more than getting a husband. They are about parents and children, the place of women in society, the role of civility, the nature of propriety and, above all, the pain and pitfalls of coming to understand something about yourself. A few words follow about these main themes, before going on to look at them in more detail and as they apply to the individual novels.

The three or four families in a country village that Jane Austen modestly says she writes about seem to have a timeless quality that makes them easily recognisable to us today. Mr Collins is not unlike a pompous teacher and we can almost hear Miss Bingley, just as some young Californian might today, say "eeugghh" at the sight of Elizabeth's muddy hem. Jane Austen is focusing her art on certain aspects of daily life with which she was familiar, drawing on her own life experience. Her novels are driven by conversation but always in groups or pairs involving women. We never actually hear Darcy advising Bingley that Jane has no lasting interest in him, or Mr Bennet and Mr Collins chatting after dinner. The politics of the time are barely touched on and, when they occasionally are, only in so far as they facilitate her story. The militia quartered on Meryton, for example, are sketched only as far as helps the plot proceed and no explanations are forthcoming about why they are there or what the local population feels about their presence. Strangely, religion rarely intervenes and religious sentiments are not on show. We never even get an account of a morning in church, even though clergymen are part of her heroines' society and Jane Austen's heroines are never motivated by religious feelings.

Jane Austen's novels are so fresh, her heroines so real to us and the worlds she creates so complete that the context in which her novels are written is not always readily apparent. The 42 years of her life, from 1775 to 1817, was a period of gigantic political and social upheaval both in Europe and the New World. They witnessed the American Declaration of Independence, the French Revolution, the publication of Tom Paine's *Rights of Man* (1791), the rise of Napoleon Bonaparte, 20 years of war with France, the battles of Trafalgar and Waterloo and a brief war with America. The foreign upheavals not only threatened Britain with invasion but also raised the spectre of social upheaval within Britain itself. In 1797-8 there were naval mutinies at Spithead and the Nore which coincided with the United Irishmen's uprising in Ireland. In 1801 the Enclosure Act disrupted the traditional patterns of the British countryside. In 1811 the madness of King George was followed by a regency in England. In the same year Luddite attacks on machinery began.

During this period the first rumblings of the Industrial Revolution were beginning. Steam power was underway, machinery was being built and roads and canals were necessary to transport the new materials. Towns were emerging where factories and slum dwellings became the breeding ground for a sense of rebellion. In 1801 Manchester's population had grown tenfold in only a quarter of a century. Where once a poor family divided its labour around the home and the landlord's fields, part of a complex social hierarchy, now men, women and children were becoming part of the unenfranchised masses, going out to work for capitalists whose interests lay in keeping the poor powerless. Change was also taking place in the countryside, with steel-tipped ploughs and machines for sowing seeds reducing the need for peasant farmers.

On one level, there are few signs in Austen's novels that she was in any way aware of the momentous changes going on about her and this may lead to the mistaken impression that unlike, say, the Brontës,

Jane Austen was unable to transcend the limitations of her social class or to recognise its ills and injustices. The often quoted passages about a "little bit (two inches wide) of ivory on which I work with so fine a brush", and "three or four families in a country village is the very thing to work on", both from her letters, are used to demonstrate the author's own admission of her limitations. This, though, is to mishear her irony and misread her stories. Jane Austen takes those three or four families and demonstrates, through their shallowness and vanities, exactly what is wrong with her society. On another level, Austen, whose cousin's husband, the Comte de Feuillide, was executed in 1794 during the French Revolution, is aware of social and political issues. The new class of manufacturers and traders are clearly present in her novels by way of Bingley, the Lucas family and Mrs Elton and an aspect of adventure capitalism can be seen in Sir Thomas Bertram's need to leave home and sort out his affairs in Antigua.

In a period of enormous social change, when wealth was no longer necessarily determined by the amount of land one owned and when just across the English Channel those who once wielded power by means of their property were being guillotined, respect for ownership of property of all kinds became ever more important. The need for rules to establish respect for property saw a huge increase in the number of laws making crime against property a capital offence. Respect for the rights of the moneyed classes was vital if members of these moneyed classes were not to go the way of their French peers while, on a more personal level than the law which made theft a hanging offence, the ruling classes needed the respect and deference of the lower classes. Enlightened self-interest suggested they needed to earn this respect by their duty of care for those beneath them and this comes to mind at that moment in *Persuasion* when Anne's father, leaving his stately home for Bath, expects the local working folk to turn out to wave him a heartbroken and fond farewell. None of them, it is implied, wish to do that because he has manifestly failed in his duty of care to them. Anne, however, does receive the respect of a grateful populace. This relationship, once accepted as the norm, became vital. The propertied elite needed to show care and respect for those whose lives they affected if they wanted to avoid those under them from rising up and taking a bigger share of the national cake. Perhaps just such a threat from the masses intrudes when Harriet is harried by travellers in *Emma* or when in *Northanger Abbey* there is a brief discussion of riots in London.

In a seminal study of Jane Austen, Tony Tanner points out that at some stage during this period the nature of the word 'propriety' altered, taking in this new need for respect for one's superiors. Its earlier meaning concerns the right to ownership and in Johnson's dictionary it is "peculiarity of possession: exclusive right", but the Oxford English dictionary shows how by 1782 it had also acquired the sense of "conformity with good manners". What happened, sometime around the late 18th century, is that respect for property rights and the notion of good manners became contiguous.

For Jane Austen, this ideal relationship between the landowning classes and the rural peasantry was crucial and it formed the basis of the society that she loved: the small village community where the various trades were carried out by skilled, independent artisans, where tenant farmers worked the land for their own profit and for the benefit of the landowner and where the landowner looked after those who were sick or unable to work, improved his lands by planting trees or draining fields, and where the village clergyman looked after the spiritual needs of the community. Where this relationship fails there is sure to be trouble. In *Mansfield Park*, Mr Rushton's improvements are foolish and damaging and the moral collapse of the Big House reaches a peak when Sir Thomas Bertram leaves his estates to go out to Antigua. In *Persuasion* we have the abandonment of his duties by Sir Walter and the adoption of them by the respectable and admirable Crofts. The cruelty of General Tilney in *Northanger Abbey* is matched by his wanton destruction of his community and this is set against clergyman Henry Tilney's village of Woodston where a thriving community exists with the parsonage house at its centre, simple and as yet unadorned by General Tilney's plans for improvement. The final unfinished novel, *Sanditon*, has figures who have left their home, driving they know not where, and who are trying to force a new community into being.

What, in terms of what Jane Austen valued, was the role of unpropertied women in her 18th-century world? Looking around her, she would have seen no women artists beyond a few writers, no businesswomen, no female politicians or factory owners – only daughters, wives, widows and spinsters. If the values of this society determined that social control and cohesion should rest on propriety – a conflation of manners and property rights – then what part would a woman have to play in the conduct of this society? The answer was manners. Any power that Jane Austen's heroines do possess resides in this area of good conduct. Austen's novels examine, to a supremely critical level, what exactly is meant by manners. Her dowry-free heroines, after all, have nothing else to contribute. On the other hand, someone like Emma, the heiress with her own little bit of power, has to learn the value of good manners and she learns by experiencing what happens when – by not respecting the class of the poverty-stricken Bateses and by attempting to lift a love-child of no status at all into her own society – she loses sight of their importance.

The powerlessness of women is reflected in terms of transport and movement, an aspect of society that receives a lot of attention in Austen's novels. The size, condition and availability of a family's transport says everything about them, as Mrs Elton's repeated reminders of her sister's barouche landau makes clear. In *Sense and Sensibility*, the sisters have no means of getting about unless a man or a woman of wealth offers them a ride. Elizabeth Bennet is forced to walk miles across muddy fields to visit her sister, coming under serious criticism for doing so, and she must remain with Charlotte until transport is arranged for her return home. She is only able to visit Darcy's home because she is offered a ride by her relatives. Fanny is even more circumscribed. She is left in Portsmouth for want of transport home, is left out of trips and can only ride for exercise because of the good will of her cousin Edmund. When, in *Northanger Abbey*, Catherine Morland finds herself expelled from her friends' house, she is suddenly thrown at the mercy of public transport and barely knows how she finally arrives at home. Her abandonment without a safe means of transport is worse than her expulsion from the house.

This inability to act informs every aspect of the lives of the women in the novels and it is reflected in the transitive aspect of the verbs often used to describe women. Verbs of inaction – watching, wondering, hoping, waiting – are common and the harshest, or boldest, thing one of the heroines may do to a man is cast a look at him. The list of women in the novels who, because of their lack of a husband are immobilised, is a long one – Miss Bates, Miss Fairfax, Mrs Smith, all the heroines bar possibly Emma, the heroines' unmarried sisters, even Miss Bingley has to connive and wrangle to get a life for herself while the super-confident and relatively independent Mary Crawford still has to find friendly relatives with whom she can live.

Activity determines the moral standing of the women in the novels. Elizabeth, Emma, Fanny, Elinor, Anne, all move or act within strict boundaries, waiting for men to provide transport, sitting in drawing rooms, embroidering, screen making, entertaining, providing, caring. Those women who go beyond these activities are often suspect. Lady Bertram's indolence is as damaging as her sister's activity and interference; Anne Elliot's sister feigns illness in order to draw attention to herself while Louisa Musgrove's excitability and activity cause her near death. In *Mansfield Park*, when all the characters wander beyond the bounds of the Big House across the ha ha, it becomes emblematic of the degeneration and moral collapse of the community.

Occasionally, women are able to move beyond their narrow confines without damaging the fabric of society. In *Persuasion*, her final completed novel and in some ways the most interesting of them all, there are several women who are able to live strong, confident, unencumbered lives. Nurse Rooke, who attends Anne Elliot's friend Mrs Smith, is able to live independently. Mrs Croft, the admiral's wife, is admired by Anne for her ability to take an active and equal part in her marriage, and Mrs Harville is able to take charge of Louisa Musgrove and all her panicking friends after the accident at Lyme. It is interesting that all these characters appear in the final completed novel, and are quite minor figures. One wonders what the next heroine after Anne Elliot might have been.

For a writer who accepts the structures of her society as strongly as does Jane Austen, there are some strange exceptions to her view of a quiet yet moral rural community where hierarchy and a respect and care for the feelings of others determines the good in society. One of these anomalies can be seen in the various parents who inhabit her world. With very few exceptions, they are seriously lacking in the skills needed to teach their daughters good behaviour. Mr and Mrs Bennet enjoy no understanding or sense of how to bring up their daughters: the father retires into his study and to irony while Mrs Bennet, regardless of propriety, forces her daughters at every young man who comes their way. The Dashwood's father inconveniently dies leaving them at the mercy of a weak-minded brother and scheming sister-in-law while their mother shares all Marianne's attractive but impractical sensibilities. Emma's father is a professional invalid. Fanny's parents are beyond the pale while Edmund Bertram's parents, in their very different ways, have given up their stewardship to a malicious interloper. Anne's father is perhaps the worst of all the parents due to the harm he causes, while Lady Russell, her substitute mother, does little better when it comes to sound advice on who to marry and why. Only Catherine Morland's parents cannot be criticised and then perhaps only because they have so little to do in the novel. All Austen's heroines learn their wisdom through their experiences or from their future husbands and it is strange, in a world of incompetent parents and largely stupid siblings, that creatures as bright and undamaged as Fanny, Elizabeth, Anne or Elinor emerge at all.

If, to keep the chaos of class war at bay, the ideology of late 18th-century England required good manners then this was something Jane Austen clearly bought into. It is often all her heroines have in the way of action. But are good manners as shallow as this? Do they amount to no more than a cloak for keeping the poor in their place, maintaining respect for wealth, rank and property without resorting to the heavy-handedness of authoritarianism? In Jane Austen's first effort at a complete novel, *Lady Susan*, a truly evil, but perfectly courteous woman manipulates the good manners of her relations into almost ruining her daughter's life and that of the young man she was trying to inveigle into a loveless marriage. Clearly there is more to manners than keeping your mouth closed while you are eating or saying thank you when handed your teacup. Tony Tanner, quoting Goethe, refers to a "politeness of the heart" and this is a valuable term to keep in mind when considering the deeper significance that Austen attaches to the concept of good manners. Her novels examine this inward politeness, seeing this respect for other people as essentially what holds society together. Her novels are full of people – think of Mrs Elton, Mr Collins, Marianne and Elinor's sister-in-law, Lucy Steele, Miss Bingley – whose conduct outwardly passes for politeness but whose self-aggrandising, often vicious and duplicitous talk reveals the true state of their hearts. Jane Austen's heroines come to learn the value of meaningful, truthful talk, though their moral adventures begin in ignorance of the true proprieties. Their stories are about how they learn the enduring reality of good manners. Elizabeth Bennet, Emma Woodhouse, Catherine Morland and Marianne Dashwood all learn the importance of useful talk and, if none is useful, learn to appreciate the virtue of silence.

Jane Austen's novels are played out in a public space and, as Henry Tilney points out, "every man is surrounded by a neighbourhood of voluntary spies". Rarely do her heroines have intimate, free-flowing conversations where their true feelings can be expressed, or have access to a private place where they can be alone. Manners are a public code of conduct and Elizabeth and Darcy's courtship is played out in a public space where those with eyes to see can comment on its progress; Anne and Wentworth must conduct their reconciliation under the pretence of a walk around the streets and Emma lives in a social space where everyone knows everybody else's business. Except in certain circumstances – between sisters confiding after a ball, between well-established friends in exceptional circumstances and, very occasionally, between married couples – privacy is a kind of social crime. Marianne and Willoughby's private moments cause her later heartache and disgrace, Jane Fairfax and Frank Churchill's secret engagement is socially unacceptable, Lucy Steele's confidences to Elinor are both false and hurtful. Secrecy is a step away from privacy and it too causes harm, as is shown by General Tilney's real motives in befriending Catherine, by Elizabeth keeping the secret of Wickham's true nature from her family and friends, Miss Bingley and Darcy keeping Jane's presence in London a secret from Bingley and by Mr Elliot's deceptions.

A beginning and an end, apparently simple, straightforward storytelling, very little imagery, few descriptions of surroundings – Austen's novels seem to be all surface, narratives about landed gentry talking to one another.

The distinctive style of the novels lies in the space between the conversations, in the author's ability to move seamlessly from one point of view to another without giving any overt indication of what she is doing. The story, narrated at first by an omniscient narrator, shifts without warning into the thought processes and opinions of one of her characters, and then, without warning again, into those of another. The humour and irony often lies with the reader being alert to spotting these subtle shifts and following the movement from accepting at face value what we are being told to believe to being presented with the self-deceptions of one of the characters. In the three early novels, *Sense and Sensibility*, *Pride and Prejudice* and *Northanger Abbey*, this subtlety is less well developed because the author is clearly there with us, often stepping aside from the story to deliver a crushing attack on one of her characters and then smoothly moving on. In these early works, the author hops gaily from one character's skewed vision of the world to another, setting out the foibles of individuals as if they were objective truth and daring the reader to misunderstand the irony. In the later novels the author's hand is more subtle, rarely stepping in, leaving instead the reader to find his or her own way of understanding the characters.

Jane Austen's early writings were plays and epistolary novels and the influence of these forms of writing can be seen clearly in the novels. Dialogue makes up a large part of the novels and creates much of the humour as she allows the characters to expose themselves in their own words. Since, for most of the novels, we follow the actions of the heroine, letters serve to fill in actions which take place outside her sphere of activity. Letters also put a point of view across, such as the one which Darcy writes to Elizabeth after she refuses him. He retells the entire story so far, from a very different perspective to the one with which we have previously been presented. Letters also allow characters to expose themselves, as do the letters from Miss Bingley to Jane. The exception to this is *Emma*, for here we follow the rather boring lives of a few characters who rarely go anywhere and have no need to write letters, and the few letters in the novel are rarely presented to us to read but instead are reported by their recipients.

Another aspect of Jane Austen's style is her use of caricature. Most of the novels contain these caricatures, objects of fun for readers, whose one or two distinguishing features are recognisable as elements of real people. Mr Collins, Lady Catherine, Lydia, Mrs Bennet in *Pride and Prejudice*; the laughing Charlotte and Nancy Steele in *Sense and Sensibility*; Mrs Norris, Mr Rushworth and Lady Bertram in *Mansfield Park*; Miss Bates, Mrs Elton, Mr Woodhouse in *Emma*; Admiral Croft, Sir Walter and Louisa Musgrove in *Persuasion*, all have important roles to play in their respective novels. While we recognise them for the caricature that they are, the characters in the novel must take them more seriously. While we can laugh at Mr Collins, he causes Elizabeth real distress with his proposal of marriage, and while we recognise the exaggerations of Mrs Norris, she is responsible for much of Fanny's suffering. Behind the caricature, a serious point is being made by Austen as she shows us how this type of person, albeit destructive and hurtful, are tolerated in a society where they can exploit the rules and customs. It is because they obey the rules of the game, observing a superficial politeness and keeping within the accepted bounds of their role in society, that they get away with their cruelties and wield power over those less fortunate than themselves. In Mr Collins' and Mrs Elton's case, though, both bring a certain domestic contentment to those that they marry and such caricatures remain largely peripheral to the main issues of the novel in which they appear. Other caricatures are benign and some of them, such as Miss Bates in *Emma* occasionally display more fully-rounded features, sensitivities that no Dickens caricature is capable of, often surprising the reader out of their complacency, their feeling that they know where this story is going.

A Quiet Life

Jane Austen was born in the winter of 1775 into a family that lived a quiet, ordered life. She was the sixth child and second daughter of a fairly well-to-do clergyman and his wife, both members of the gentry, her mother distantly related to a duke. The family lived in Steventon, a village of about 30 families in Hampshire, in a large parsonage house with dairy cows, hens and a vegetable garden providing much of their food, and the father supplementing his income by taking in boarding pupils. As an infant, like all her siblings, Jane was boarded out with a local family; a not unusual practice at the time, among those that could afford it, and once she returned home she lived in an over-full house, sharing a bedroom with her older sister Cassandra. The family read widely, particularly seeking out the relatively new literary form of the novel. In 1783, at the age of seven, Jane was sent away from home again, this time with Cassandra, to study with a

Mrs Cawley. A brief two years back at home, following a dangerous illness, and Jane left home again, this time for Reading and a school for young ladies. Some time during her teenage years she turned her interest in reading into writing and she wrote a series of plays, a satirical history of England and, her first effort at novel writing, *Lady Susan*.

> ### *Lady Susan*
> Probably in 1793, when she was about 18, Jane Austen sat down to write her first novel. It was written, in an epistolary form which was common at that period, as a series of letters between the Lady of the title and her friends, and between the people on whom Lady Susan was preying. Unlike Jane Austen's later heroines, even unlike her later villains, Lady Susan is just plain wicked. The novel's plot centres around a scheming widow who seeks to marry off her unloved and unlooked-after daughter to a dolt while attempting to acquire a much younger and wealthier man for herself. Her plots fail, the eligible young man she had her sights on marries her daughter and Lady Susan is exposed for the schemer that she truly is. What is strange about the novel is that Jane Austen clearly enjoys her evil protagonist, who has the energy and wit of Elizabeth Bennet or Mary Crawford, while those who represent models of propriety are simply boring. In this novel too, behaviour which is only hinted at in her later novels, such as adultery, is openly admitted by Lady Susan. Significantly, there is no moral ending and Lady Susan remains unrepentant. The complexity of an attractive but bad woman is returned to in *Mansfield Park*, where again it causes some problems both for the reader and perhaps the writer. *Lady Susan* is brief and ends with a conclusion that has the author stepping in to explain the fates of her characters and why the letters stop. Jane Austen never offered *Lady Susan* for publication but she did take the trouble, ten years later, of writing out a fair copy so presumably it meant something to her.

As she grew into a young woman, Jane's older brothers gradually left home, one, Francis, to the East Indies, one to study at Oxford and one to become a curate. The oldest brother, George, never returned home from being boarded out as a baby; it is thought that he was probably handicapped in some way and remained all his long life away from the rest of the family. The second eldest, Edward, had been adopted by childless, wealthy relations and was to inherit landed property. He spent his time, like Darcy or Tom Bertram must have done, waiting to come into his inheritance.

For Jane and her sister there were no careers to be had, except as wives, and the chances of a good marriage for girls who had neither stunning good looks or a large dowry were poor. In addition, the biting wit, evident to us in in Jane's letters, may well have put off a few men hoping for a quiet domestic life. There were romances however. Her sister Cassandra became engaged to a penniless curate who went off to the West Indies in 1795 as chaplain to a regiment. By the age of 20, having seen the futures of her older brothers and her sister sorted out, Jane had few prospects. She attended local balls and soirées, contemporaries call her a flirt, and, like Charlotte in *Pride and Prejudice*, she must have known that meeting someone at these balls and social events were her best chance of obtaining a home and a life of her own. She began writing a novel called *Elinor and Marianne*, a first draft of what was to become *Sense and Sensibility*.

Like Elizabeth Bennet and Elinor Dashwood, as long as their father lived Jane and Cassandra were secure. Jane had an allowance of £20 a year – about £1500 in modern terms – out of a family income of what today would be around £40,000. Although neither Jane nor Cassandra had any other means of support, neither ever considered taking up work as a governess or companion. Beginning in 1794, the sisters spent many of their summers staying with the family of their wealthy brother Edward in Kent and it was here that Jane experienced both what it was like to live in luxury and what it was like to be a relatively poor relation. It is probable that Edward's mother-in-law, Mrs Knight, gave Jane some cash whenever she visited, although Edward's wife Elizabeth preferred Cassandra, whose wit may well have been a little less severe. There are echoes of this not quite comfortable relationship – the snobbery and lack of sensitivity of the wealthy, the feelings of the poor relation – in many of the novels. Decades later, Jane's favourite niece, Fanny, Edward's daughter, wrote disparagingly about her aunt Jane:

> ... it is very true that Aunt Jane from various circumstances was not so *refined* as she ought to have been from her *talent*, & if she had but lived 50 years later she would have been in many respects more suitable to our *refined* tastes. They were not rich & the people around them with whom they chiefly mixed, were not at all high bred, or in short anything more than *mediocre & they* of course tho' superior in mental powers & *cultivation* were on the same level so far as *refinement* goes – But I think in later life their intercourse with Mrs Knight (who was very fond of & kind to them) improved them both & Aunt Jane was too clever not to put aside all possible signs of 'commonness' (if such an expression is allowable) & teach herself to be more refined, at least in intercourse with people in general. Both the Aunts were brought up in the most complete ignorance of the World & its ways (I mean as to fashion &c) & if it had not been for Papa's marriage which brought them into Kent & the kindness of Mrs Knight who used often to have one or other of the sisters staying with her, they would have been, tho' not less clever and agreeable in themselves, very much below par as to good society & its ways.

This piece of writing could so easily be transposed into *Emma* for Mrs Elton to write about her neighbours or to *Pride and Prejudice* for Miss Bingley to write about Elizabeth.

Then, in 1796 and at the age of 20, Jane fell in love with Tom Lefroy, a wealthy Anglo-Irish law student. Despite Jane writing to her sister that she would accept his imminent proposal, his family put an end to the brief flirtation. Lefroy eventually married an heiress and became Lord Chief Justice of Ireland. In the spring of 1797, as Cassandra prepared for her wedding, news came that her fiancé had died at sea of yellow fever. The two sisters found themselves without prospects. Cassandra's fiancé had left her £1,000, (about £70,000 today), a sum that would just about earn enough interest for her to scrape a living from, as long as there was also some support from her father. Jane was growing older and no prettier or financially better endowed and she began to notice that at the local balls she was often a wallflower: "I do not think I am very much in request – people are rather apt not to ask me until they could not help it ..." Jane began the first draft of *First Impressions*, the original of *Pride and Prejudice*.

No letters survive from the year 1797, which must have been one of the lowest points of Jane Austen's life. Both sisters' prospects were destroyed, their brothers were all gone, their father looking towards retirement. In that year Jane's father wrote to the publishers Thomas Cadell suggesting that they might like to consider publishing *First Impressions*. They declined the offer. Undeterred, or possibly unaware that the approach had been made, Jane turned to a new novel, entitled *Susan*, which would eventually metamorphose into *Northanger Abbey*. During these years, towards the end of her father's working life, Jane and her sister, both by now emerging as established spinsters, were often separated, one or the other of them visiting relatives. Jane, by now aged around her mid twenties, was called on regularly to attend sisters-in-law's confinements, help out with children and enjoy the benefits of wealthier, more fulfilled lives. She and her sister wrote regularly, and many of the letters survive, although some which might have shed more light on the state of Jane Austen's mind were destroyed. Judging by some of the comments in her letters it is understandable, perhaps, that it was Cassandra who was invited to relatives more often than her sister. The comments that Jane Austen makes about her neighbours' clothes and behaviour were intended for Cassandra's eyes only and many can only be described as pure bitchiness: "Mrs Hall of Sherbourne was brought to bed yesterday of a dead child, some weeks before she expected, owing to a fright – I suppose she happened, unawares, to look at her husband."

Jane travelled, spending time with uncles and aunts at Bath and in London, and with her brother in Kent. Her mother, writing to her son James' new wife in 1797, before the news of Cassandra's fiancé's death had reached them, said: "I look forward to you as a real comfort to me in my old age, when Cassandra is gone into Shropshire & Jane – the Lord knows where." Around this time, Jane was writing *Northanger Abbey* and it is very probable that she drew on her visits to Bath as material for her novel. When completed, *Northanger Abbey* was put away in a drawer and stayed there for four years. Her own mother was becoming an invalid, and Jane had to look after her needs, doling out her laudanum and taking charge of the house for periods of time.

In 1801, Jane's father retired from his living, giving it up to his son James. His only responsibilities now were to his two unmarried daughters, and one Christmas, while the two girls were away, he and his wife made plans to retire to Bath. Long after the event, accounts of Jane hearing the news say that she fainted away; she would certainly not have relished the idea of leaving all that was familiar to her and going to a place she clearly despised. It is highly likely that part of her parents' plans for the future involved the hope that one or both of their two spinster daughters would find a husband at one of the many social events in Bath. Jane Austen was 25, had already written *Pride and Prejudice*, *Sense and Sensibility* and *Northanger Abbey* although none of them were published. Her comfortable, familiar life came to an end and with it came a ten year break in her writing output. Her letters to Cassandra, covering the period of the preparations for the move, have been largely excised, perhaps by a family unwilling to let the world see just exactly what her feelings were.

The family sold up all their possessions, including Jane's piano which she had been used to playing each morning, keeping only their beds, and moved to a series of smaller and smaller rented apartments in Bath.

In 1802, Jane faced Charlotte Lucas' dilemma. While visiting old neighbours in Manydown Park, a large estate near Steventon, Jane received a proposal of marriage from its shy and none-too-bright heir, Harris Bigg Wither. She was 27, he was considerably younger, and Jane must have known that another offer was unlikely to arise. Jane accepted him. The marriage would mean financial security, independence, her own carriage, and an ease on the strained finances of her family. It would also break her close ties with her sister and, above all, involve an intimacy with a man she probably didn't love and wasn't attracted to. Jane accepted his offer but overnight she changed her mind and she and her sister left the house and returned to Bath. Harris recovered from his loss, married two years later and had a large family. Jane returned to genteel poverty in Bath, a place she hated.

In 1803 *Northanger Abbey* or *Susan* as it then was, was accepted for publication but then shelved by the publisher, Crosby.

Without her piano or the countryside she had grown up in, Jane took to walking the streets around Bath, visiting relatives in Lyme Regis and other resorts and began another novel, *The Watsons*.

> ### The Watsons
> A fragment of about 17,000 words, *The Watsons* was written while Jane was living in Bath and was abandoned around the time of her father's death. It is very different in tone from her earlier works – the Watson family is much lower class than even the Bennets, have only the one maid, and an elderly horse and carriage. The father is an invalid, about to die and the sisters have no prospects. Emma, its heroine, had been adopted by a wealthy aunt whose recent remarriage has sent her with no prospects for a future inheritance back to her family. Emma attends a ball, meets the three men who she might marry in the course of the novel and talks to her brother and sisters. It is clear, from a letter that Cassandra Austen wrote, that Emma was to be dependent on an unpleasant sister-in-law after her father's death, and to receive a proposal from the wealthy Lord Osborne, which she would refuse in favour of the hand of the humbler clergyman, Mr Howard. What is interesting is that the Watson family seem so much more vivid than families in her other novels. Elizabeth Bennet's sisters, by comparison, do not really come to life or do very much, while in *The Watsons* we see the sisters bickering over sharing bedrooms, laying the table and doing the family wash. It is not known why the novel was never completed but perhaps it came a little too close to autobiography with its discussions of the need to marry, the interactions of the siblings and its details of just getting by on an everyday basis.

In 1895, her father died. Jane, Cassandra and their mother were now in a parlous state, with Cassandra's and their mother's two tiny incomes and Jane penniless. The brothers made some financial contributions and the women found rented accommodation, for the first four years in Southampton, close to the brother Francis, a naval officer, and then in Chawton in Hampshire. Here they lived in a cottage consisting of six bedrooms, a garden and outhouses, and with the services of a cook, a manservant and a maid (but no carriage). All this was funded by Jane's brother Edward, who for all his wealth had seen fit not to help the three women for the four years following his father's death. Jane again had a permanent home, and a piano, and could return to the kind of country lifestyle that she loved. A fourth woman came to join them in their cottage, a family friend who was also a spinster, and they fell into a routine of housekeeping, gardening and visiting with their neighbours. Jane had a place to write and a shared bedroom with her sister. Brothers and their families were regular visitors and several of them lived nearby.

Jane began a typical day by playing her piano and organising the family breakfast before sitting down to work at her writing desk. Dinner usually took place in the middle of the afternoon and was followed by social activities like visiting a neighbour or playing a card game or reading her day's writing aloud. Jane wrote a rather cross letter to Crosby asking for *Susan* back and threatening to take it to another publisher. In reply they threatened legal action and offered to sell the manuscript back to her for £10, a sum she could not muster.

First Impressions and *Elinor and Marianne* were taken out and revised and the latter, renamed *Sense and Sensibility*, was sent to a publisher, Egerton's of Whitehall, in 1810. They agreed to publish it, at the author's expense and on the understanding that if the book failed to sell, the author would have to meet the publisher's expenses also. Jane's brother Henry lent her the money and the publication proceeded. Published anonymously, it received good reviews and the first edition of 1000 copies sold out with a profit for Jane of £200.

Pride and Prejudice followed in 1813 and this time Egerton bought the copyright for £110. It was an immediate success. Her literary success did not ease the sharpness of her tongue in any way and in a letter of 14 October 1814 we read:

> Only think of Mrs Holder's being dead! Poor woman, she has done the only thing in the world she could possibly do to make one cease to abuse her.

In 1814 *Mansfield Park* followed and, although it sold out in six months, its reception was not as ecstatic as for *Pride and Prejudice*. Even at the turn of the 19th century Fanny Price must have been a bit difficult to love. By the following year word had leaked out who the author of these three novels was and she had become so popular that the Prince Regent decided he would like to have her next novel dedicated to him. *Emma* was published in 1815 by John Murray, Egerton having annoyed her over refusing to reprint *Mansfield Park*. *Persuasion* was started in August 1815 and *Northanger Abbey* bought back from its publisher and revised for publication. By 1816, feeling a little ill and tired, she was completing *Persuasion*. Unsatisfied with it, and probably intending to work on it some more she put it aside and began her final work, *Sanditon*. After 12 chapters, illness forced her to stop writing. She wrote her will and died in July 1817.

1

Northanger Abbey

Northanger Abbey, Austen's first novel to be accepted by a publisher, was probably written between 1798 and 1799. The author had spent part of 1798 visiting Bath with her uncle, James Leigh Perrot, and his wife. Another aunt, Mrs Cooke, had just published a Gothic novel whose heroine experiences many of the trials of other Gothic heroines and Jane would most probably have been called on to read it.

Northanger Abbey is a satire on two current fashions in novel writing and each of the novel's two volumes satirise one of these, the first volume providing a parody of the romance novel and the second a satire on the Gothic novel. Both of these genres concern themselves either directly or through metaphor with the *rite de passage* of a young woman into maturity. In the first volume of *Northanger Abbey*, Jane Austen draws on the work of romantic novelists such as Fanny Burney and there are clear parallels between Burney's heroine Camilla, of the novel of the same name, and Catherine, the heroine of *Northanger Abbey*. In *Camilla* an artless, virtuous, innocent heroine, just at a marriageable age, leaves home under the guardianship of a wealthy, kind but incompetent surrogate parent whose heir she is to be. In *Northanger Abbey*, Catherine is assumed to be the Allens' heir by both John Thorpe and General Tilney. Camilla has a vacuous cousin, who provides a parallel for the role of Isabella Thorpe, and Camilla's false, ignorant suitor finds an echo in the pestering of Catherine for a time by John Thorpe. Camilla's life lessons are taught her by a suitor and mentor, although in her case a boring but worthy one, unlike the lively Henry Tilney.

While in Bath, Catherine is drawn into the attractions of the Gothic novel. The plots of these novels follow similar lines. Set often in medieval times and in fantastical settings of medieval castles, secret tunnels, tombs and hidden panels, they involve death, mystery and the supernatural. Their protagonist is a virtuous, wealthy but lost, high-born maiden who must solve the mystery in the plot and recover her family and her inheritance. In Volume II, as a bathetic parallel to all of this, Catherine too visits an ancient building, encounters secret compartments, fears the murder of an innocent and explores forbidden rooms. The real threats to Catherine, of a much more mundane variety than those of the plots of her favourite reading, come in the form of a greedy, self-aggrandising man, and gossip.

This self-conscious engagement with the structure of the genre in which she is writing takes other forms than the play with plot and character. An unusual element here is the nature of the author's presence in the novel. In her other novels, Austen is happy to deliver a quick character assassination as the omniscient narrator and then move on to the interior workings of her heroines' psyches. But here, where her heroine's interior conversations with herself are so lacking, we have instead, like Fanny Burney or Samuel Richardson, the most popular of the writers in the romantic genre, the author stepping into the pages of the novel. The plot is stopped for half a page and she addresses the reader directly, as if the author is standing at the side of the stage and explaining herself to us, delivering little tongue-in-cheek homilies. So, in Chapter 5 of Volume I, we have the author, using the first person singular, teasingly upbraiding the world, suspected to be mostly made up of secret novel readers, of denigrating a genre in which "the greatest powers of the mind are displayed, in which the most thorough knowledge of human nature, the happiest delineation of its varieties, the liveliest effusions of wit and humour are conveyed to the world in the best chosen language." Here, unlike the works of Richardson, who in his epic tome *Sir Charles Grandison* provided an index to the homilies so that those in need of an ethical or spiritual fix could turn straight to the right page, Austen's messages come in dense, defensive layers of irony. In Chapter 10, as Catherine falls asleep wondering which of her dresses she should wear to the next day's outing, we hear the cynical homily on dress which concludes: "Woman is fine for her own satisfaction alone. No man will admire her the more, no woman will like her the better for it." Later, the author throws in another almost sardonic remark: "To come with a well informed mind, is to come with an inability of administering to the vanity of others, which a sensible person would always wish to avoid. A woman especially, if she have the misfortune of knowing anything, should conceal it as well as she can." (Vol. I, Ch. 14).

There are many such instances of the author engaging the reader in a discussion of what the novel is to be about and, indeed, the reader's introduction to Catherine is couched in a discussion of whether or not she is truly a heroine. Catherine, though she seems at first to be entirely unsuited to that role, when compared to the heroines of the Gothic novel, becomes a truly modern heroine, learning about the real world through a series of feasible trials which mirror and provide a counterpoint to the world of fiction. Towards the end of the novel, Austen steps in again, pointing out how few pages the reader has left, discussing the appropriateness of introducing a new character in the final pages of the book, teasing us with the information that it was this new character's laundry list that Catherine found and instructing us to find him the most wonderful young man in all the world.

Northanger Abbey, then, plays with the reader's expectations of romance and Gothic horror and self-consciously discusses the very nature of a relatively new area of literature, the novel. It also offers us the real story that Austen wishes to tell us, a tale about poor parenting, the trials of finding a place and a voice in the world and, a particular difficulty when setting out on life's journey, learning how to differentiate duplicitous talk from politeness of the heart.

The characters in *Northanger Abbey* are clearly drawn in parody of the stock characters of romantic and Gothic fiction. Eleanor is the beautiful, orphaned, badly-treated young woman, Catherine the young girl who must explore the ruined house and discover the evil plot, John Thorpe the wicked seducer who carries the heroine off in his carriage away from the safety of her friends, Mrs Allen the foolish guardian who allows her charge to fall into danger, Isabella the duplicitous friend who plots the heroine's undoing, General Tilney the abusive parent who may have been responsible for the sudden death of his wife and the incarceration in a lonely building of his beautiful daughter. Such a list could be continued but their real interest to Austen is, most ironically, their very lack of a single dimension. She tells us that life, as she understands it, is not black and white and that people are not just good, or foolish or wicked. The threats that a young girl like Catherine might encounter are both more complex and more banal than those of the heroines in the books she reads.

Like the opening line of *Pride and Prejudice*, the first sentence of this novel sets out the theme that will played out in the course of the story: "No one who had ever seen Catherine Morland in her infancy would have supposed her born to be an heroine." Catherine, of course, as the reader well knows, is going to be the heroine. The sentence starts with a negative, "no one", which is actually referring to its opposite, everyone, so we are in similar, slippery territory to that of the *Pride and Prejudice*'s "truth universally acknowledged". It is possible that Austen's singular use of the indefinite article "an" being set before the word "heroine" is deliberate, so that the reader must either linger on the word by saying it carefully or drop the 'h'. By drawing our attention to the word in this way, we are alerted to romantic fiction and its conventional heroines.

Of all Austen's heroines, Catherine seems the least sympathetic. We have little access to her thoughts, and her tendency to react to other people on a superficial level creates much of the humour but leaves the reader distanced from her. However, she is naïve but not stupid; unlike the more sophisticated Eleanor and Henry Tilney, she fails to read the signals that Isabella sends out and sees only her lively nature, but eventually comes to realise her true nature. She mishears John Thorpe's messages but knows that he is a bore and quickly dismisses him. She is aware that General Tilney creates a difficult atmosphere but cannot read the reasons why and the second half of the novel derives its fun from her assumption that such a man must have killed his wife when in fact, as Henry hints, he just made her life difficult with his demanding egotism. Most importantly, Catherine learns that it is not always good to talk. She learns that both Isabella and General Tilney may say one thing and mean another, that their talk can be deceitful and, while couched in terms of affection and concern, is really determined by their own self-absorption. In the many discussions between Henry, Eleanor and Catherine, Austen shows how the nature of real manners is instead bound up with a free flow of information and a use of talk which is not intended to deceive but to make things clearer. What is important is a politeness of the heart which keeps the two more sophisticated young people from expressing their clearer understanding to Catherine, out of respect for others and care for her feelings. The novel is concerned with the way in which, with Henry's help and some hard knocks, Catherine learns the meaning of useful talk.

As the novel opens, Catherine is described in Chapter 2 as an innocent, "her disposition cheerful and open, without conceit or affectation of any kind – her manners just removed from the awkwardness and shyness of a girl; ... and her mind about as ignorant and unformed as the female mind at seventeen usually is." Here we have the author's indication of the unformed mind that is about to embark on its Bath adventures, her only knowledge of the world a set of partially understood quotations from Pope, Thompson, Shakespeare, "looking forward to pleasures untasted and unalloyed, and free from the apprehensions of evil as from the knowledge of it." (Vol. II, Ch. 29)

What Catherine encounters on her great adventure is mindless talk and crowds of people pushing, jostling or sitting still while waiting to be asked to dance. Bath, in *Northanger Abbey*, is the antithesis of Jane Austen's ordered world. Here people "squeeze" in among a "mob", a "throng", a "struggling assembly", where Catherine must cling on to Mrs Allen for fear of being "torn asunder". For all the convenience of so many shops selling muslin, this is a lifeless society where everyone "was to be seen in the room at different periods of the fashionable hours; crowds of people were every moment passing in and out, up the steps and down; people whom nobody cared about, and nobody wanted to see ..." When Mrs Allen finally meets someone she knows, the two women's meaningless conversation is expressed in the context of a familiar aphorism – it is better to give than to receive – which is given a new, non-moral meaning: "they proceeded to make enquiries and give intelligence as to their families, sisters and cousins, both talking together, far more ready to give than to receive, and each hearing very little of what the other said." Similarly, at home, Mrs Allen "could never be entirely silent; and, therefore, while she sat at her work, if she lost her needle or broke her thread, if she heard a carriage in the street, or saw a speck upon her gown, she must observe it aloud, whether there were anyone at leisure to answer her or not."

Isabella pours out gushing untruths, learned from her reading, while her brother shouts profanities and talks only about himself, and mostly lies at that. The Tilneys, on the other hand, are aware of the value of useful, sensitive talk and, when Catherine meets Eleanor, the two women's conversation, while completely superficial in subject matter, shows consideration and mindfulness: " … though in all probability not an observation was made, nor an expression used by either which had not been made and used some thousands of times before, under that roof, in every Bath season, yet the merit of their being spoken with simplicity and truth, and without personal conceit, might be something uncommon."

Henry, by contrast, has attitude. He hates the use of the word "nice", teases Catherine about the kind of meaningless talk they must have as dancing partners, about what she will write about him in her diary, invokes the language of the Gothic novel to tease Catherine as they approach Northanger Abbey and engages in silly chat about muslin.

In many ways, Henry provides the moral compass for this novel. He shares Jane Austen's humour, her ironic distance from her society, her awareness that a gracious heart is the governing rule of good behaviour and, like Elizabeth Bennet, her ability to spot a fake. He is also a good teacher, explaining things to Catherine when he feels it will do some good and passing over other things, such as his understanding of Isabella Thorpe and her motives, because to express them might hurt her friend. In the kind of novels which Jane Austen is drawing on, like Richardson's *Sir Charles Grandison* or Burney's *Camilla* for example, the hero devotes several pages at a time to lectures on morality but Henry's teachings have a lighter touch. He offers propositions half playfully ("I consider a country dance an emblem of marriage", for example) and allows his pupil to explore them. In the conventional romantic novel, the introduction of a character like Henry might be by way of some suitable adventure, saving her from a runaway horse perhaps. Here, as if to scupper any such expectation, he is formally introduced by the master of ceremonies. He ought, in a romantic novel, to be dashingly handsome but he does not quite fill the bill: "He seemed to be about four or five and twenty, was rather tall, had a pleasing countenance, a very intelligent and lively eye, and, if not quite handsome, was very near it."

Unlike Elizabeth and the other heroines, Henry is not hog-tied by his gender. He has an income, a role in society, is able to come and go as he wishes. His acquiescence in General Tilney's movements of the family is more in respect of his sister's best interests than the kind of dependence that keeps Elizabeth at Mr Collins' house. Eventually, he assumes the authority to stand up to the bad behaviour of his father. Austen portrays Henry in terms that contrast him with the other men of the novel and, unlike these others, he shows no interest in gambling, horses, shooting or any of the other characteristically male forms of behaviour. He is even, however ironically, able to hold a conversation about the cost and durability of muslin. Henry does quite a lot of Jane Austen's work for her, introducing for the modern reader what they may not realise Catherine is expecting to find in the abbey:

> But you must be aware that when a young lady is (by whatever means) introduced into a dwelling of this kind, she is always lodged apart from the rest of the family. While they snugly repair to their own end of the house, she is formally conducted by Dorothy, the ancient housekeeper, up a different staircase, and along many gloomy passages, into an apartment never used since some cousin or kin died in it about twenty years before. Can you stand such a ceremony as this? Will not your mind misgive you when you find yourself in this gloomy chamber – too lofty and extensive for you, with only the feeble rays of a single lamp to take in its size – its walls hung with tapestry exhibiting figures as large as life, and the bed, of dark green stuff or purple velvet, presenting even a funereal appearance? Will not your heart sink within you?
> (Vol. II, Ch. 1)

It is Henry, too, who later brings Catherine back to the reality of his father's house from her Gothic fantasy concerning his mother's death. While for Mr Darcy's good nature we must depend on the testimony of his housekeeper, here, instead, is a carefully drawn, amusing man, aware of the needs of those around him and who in the final analysis marries Catherine because she loves him and not because he wants her.

While the first villain offered to us in this novel, John Thorpe, turns out to be a red herring, the real villain of the piece is, of course,

General Tilney. Here, as in *Emma*, the astute reader is aware of General Tilney's real faults long before the heroine is, although we have no prior knowledge of the harm that John Thorpe does by bragging about Catherine as a prospective wife. The Gothic fantasy that Catherine takes for reality proposes a man who has killed his wife or may have her locked up. In reality, General Tilney is an Austenian villain because his wickedness is of a social nature. His house is a model of modernity – modern plain china, industrial scale vegetable gardens, large numbers of employees, rather than tenants who work their own plots, efficient fireplaces – but in Jane Austen's eyes this only serves to reveal a lack of regard for the traditions that have kept England the kind of place she approves of. Austen values the social cohesion of a small community which depends on the good works of the paternalistic landowner and the respect of the peasant classes. Tilney's improvements are all aimed at benefiting himself rather than improving the lot of the people who work for him. His hothouse fruits out of season and his modern rooms are designed to make him look impressive in the eyes of his visitors but which, the author feels, make him unimpressive in the eyes of a discerning reader.

The example of poor parenthood that General Tilney offers, though, is a more complex one. Like the villains of the Gothic novels, he is a tyrant whose children are forced to go with him to Bath and then to Northanger. Their mealtimes, visits by friends, their movements and time, even their potential marriage partners, are all to be rendered subordinate to his wishes. He is also a deceiver. He attempts to deceive Catherine as to his intentions and his character. He has no thought to Catherine's character or qualities and she simply represents a good marriage in the form of the wealth he expects her to inherit. It is not until she is long established at the General's house that Catherine begins to notice his manner of speaking: " … why should he say one thing so positively, and mean another all the while, was most unaccountable! How were people, at that rate to be understood? Who but Henry could have been aware of what his father was at?" (Vol. II, Ch. 11). Eventually, Catherine also becomes the victim of another of the General's cruelties, his appalling rage. When he discovers that she is not the heiress he has been led to believe, he becomes "enraged with almost everybody in the world but himself" and throws her out of the house, abandoning all his responsibilities as a parent and citizen. Later, we hear of his rage at Henry's behaviour, only mollified by his daughter marrying a lord and the news that Catherine was not penniless and might well inherit the Allens' money after all. His earlier apparent politeness was not the true politeness that all Austen heroines either understand or learn in the course of their growing up.

Mrs Allen, though at a more trivial level, is equally lacking in moral awareness. She is concerned only with clothes and their upkeep and judges her acquaintances on the value and maintenance of their outfits. Her only parental attention to her temporary ward is to observe that Catherine should go out in the rain as she wants since she does not mind getting dirty. When she learns of Catherine's frightening experience finding her way home alone, she dismisses Catherine's story and moves on to the great rent made in her new dress while at Bath.

Of all the parents in the novels, the Morlands seem the most well adjusted and sensible, reacting calmly to Catherine's return in such unusual circumstances, wondering at how silly a wife she is likely to be, considering her naivety, and sensibly allowing the engagement to go ahead confident in the knowledge that things will work out eventually.

In this novel, too, the concepts of property and propriety are critically examined. The Morlands and Henry Tilney are people of relatively small income who, in their role as shepherds of their parishes, carry out their duties. These figures understand that with property comes a duty of care. General Tilney and Mrs Allen, on the other hand, have not made the connection between privilege and duty and although both of them display propriety and good manners, neither of them is able to operate at any level deeper than a superficial one.

That this novel is not about a young woman finding a husband is indicated by the actual account of the marriage: "The event which it authorised soon followed: Henry and Catherine were married, the bells rang, and everybody smiled." Jane Austen gets this necessary but unimportant event over in a terse, dismissive sentence.

Does this novel tell us anything significant about the period in which Jane Austen lived, or is the criticism that she was unable to move beyond her limited social class to the wider world of politics and political thought a genuine one? As a background to this story, we have Eleanor's mistaken idea that the new Gothic novel Catherine is talking about is actually some political upheaval in London:

> ... she immediately pictured to herself a mob of three thousand men assembling in St George's Fields, the Bank attacked, the Tower threatened, the streets of London flowing with blood, a detachment of the Twelfth Light Dragoons (the hopes of the nation) called up from Northampton to quell the insurgents, and the gallant Captain Frederick Tilney, in the moment of charging at the head of his troop, knocked off his horse by a brickbat from an upper window.
>
> (Vol. I, Ch. 14)

All of these events that Henry describes had actually taken place in London in the years preceding the publication of the novel. Later, in Vol. II, Ch. 9, we have the "neighbourhood of voluntary spies" speech where Henry describes an England where neighbours are set against one another looking for traitors. At that period the French were the Al Qaida of their time, the nation's enemy, and they, and the many working-class people creating political upheavals in the nation's capital, were seen as a serious threat to the very lives of the propertied classes. Austen does not comment on such events but neither is her novel suspended in a political vacuum.

And so, through her trip to Bath and then to Northanger Abbey, Catherine learns to distinguish true talk from lies, she learns that Isabella's gushing is all about herself, and that her professions of friendship cannot be maintained for any length of time. She learns that the Tilneys, or two of them at least, understand the real nature of talk. More importantly, Catherine learns that life is not a Gothic novel or a romance and evil can sometimes be better understood in terms of the self-serving, petty motives of respectable folk.

2

Sense and Sensibility

Letters written by her sister Cassandra, after Jane Austen's death, suggest that *Sense and Sensibility* originally came into existence as an epistolary novel called *Elinor and Marianne*, written around 1795. It was put aside for a few years while she wrote *First Impressions*, which later became *Pride and Prejudice*, and *Susan*, the first draft of *Northanger Abbey*. In its early form, the writing that became *Sense and Sensibility* may well have been an exercise in the comparison of the two antithetical concepts of the title: one sister, Elinor, displaying and exhorting her sister to good sense, while the other wrote effusively about her great feelings and how she lets them rule her behaviour. Other novels had been published in a similar vein. We have no way of knowing what Jane Austen's take on that debate might have been but the novel which eventually emerged was much more complex than the simple oppositions suggested by its title. *Sense and Sensibility*, like *Northanger Abbey*, takes a current literary tradition, that of setting antithetical concepts together in order to deliver a homily on the virtues of one and the vices of the other, and stands it on its head. The result is that there is much that is attractive in the sensibilities of Marianne and much to be annoyed about in the good sense of her sister.

The word 'sensibility' is ambivalent in its meanings. Used positively, it can indicate delicacy of feeling, a strong sense of morality and, in its most refined sense, a Zen-like composure which comes through true understanding. Characters dominated by their sensibilities would understand, one assumes, how best to behave because they would be sensible to the feelings of those around them. The word also, however, carries suggestions of fragility, so that the sensibilities of individuals could expose them to the harshness of others and the cruelties of the world. At its extreme manifestation, sensibility turns to hysteria as the fragile sensibilities of the individual are destroyed by the cruelty they see around them. *Sense and Sensibility* is littered with the casualties of this latter meaning of the world sensibility: Marianne, Willoughby, the two Elizabeths and, to a lesser extent, Edward, Brandon, Mrs Dashwood.

But the other human quality, sense, also carries layers of meaning. The person with sense deals with the world according to logic, not emotion. This has its drawbacks. When Lucy Steele abandons one brother and marries the other, she is acting with great sense because she will spend the rest of her life without financial worries and be able to indulge her every whim. The novel is full of marriages made out of good sense, yet none of them exhibit any happiness or depth.

The novel deals with, among other things, this debate between sense and sensibility but only a very superficial account would suggest that Marianne is the embodiment of sensibility and Elinor sense, or that one of these qualities prevails over the other in the resolution of the novel.

Very early on in *Sense and Sensibility*, we are instructed by the opening description of the two sisters as to the route this novel is to take:

> Elinor ... possessed a strength of understanding and coolness of judgement, which qualified her, though only nineteen, to be the counsellor of her mother, and enabled her frequently to counteract, to the advantage of them all, that eagerness of mind in Mrs Dashwood which must generally have led to imprudence. She had an excellent heart; – her disposition was affectionate, and her feelings were strong, but she knew how to govern them ...
>
> Marianne's abilities were, in many respects, quite equal to Elinor's. She was sensible and clever; but eager in everything; her sorrows, her joys, could have no moderation. She was generous, amiable, interesting: she was everything but ...
>
> (Vol. I, Ch. 1)

Later, through the eyes of Willoughby, we find that their physical appearance reflects their personal qualities:

> Miss Dashwood had a delicate complexion, regular features, and a remarkably pretty figure. Marianne was still handsomer. Her form, though not so correct as her sister's, in having the advantage of height, was more striking ...
>
> (Vol. I, Ch. 10)

Marianne responds to events and people through her emotions. She refuses to accept that her conduct should be anything other than an expression of her true feelings. Her sister recognises the need to put up barriers between her feelings and those she encounters, suppressing her irritation at ignorance or crassness out of respect for those around her and in order to protect herself:

> Marianne was silent; it was impossible for her to say what she did not feel, however trivial the occasion; and upon Elinor therefore the whole task of telling lies when politeness required it, always fell.
>
> (Vol. I, Ch. 21)

The sisters' differences of temperament can be seen reflected in the choice of men with whom they fall in love. Edward Ferrars is diffident, undemonstrative, graceless, plain, sensible and bent on a quiet domestic life. Willoughby, by way of contrast, is carefree, gay, an excellent actor (a trait shared by Henry Crawford in *Mansfield Park*) and careless of social niceties – visiting the house he is to inherit, giving Marianne the horse, his obvious attentions to her – while its suits him to be, at least. He is finally exposed as the spineless, gold-digging, seducer of innocents, while Edward emerges as the loyal, even to the point of suffering an unhappy marriage, thoughtful and steady husband.

The differences between the sisters are laid out for the reader in a series of set pieces in which it is often unclear where Austen's sympathies lie. One such is the debate in Vol. I, Ch. 18 between the sisters and Edward about how the countryside is to be appreciated. With Elinor's tacit approval, Edward disclaims any understanding of the picturesque and claims, quite straightforwardly, that he prefers straight trees to crooked ones, and occupied farm houses with cultivated gardens to ruins and weeds. Marianne, looking forward to the day when he will, she supposes, be her brother-in-law, looks at her sister in sympathy.

Earlier, Marianne eulogises the beauty of falling leaves and receives a sardonic reply from her sister:

> "With what transporting sensations have I formerly seen them fall! How delighted, as I walked to see them driven in showers about me by the wind! What feelings have they, the season, the air altogether inspired! Now there is no-one to regard them. They are seen only as a nuisance, swept hastily off, and driven, as much as possible from the sight."
> "It is not everyone," said Elinor, "who has your passion for dead leaves."
>
> (Vol. I, Ch. 14)

While Marianne can sing and play, Elinor's great talent is in screen-making, a metaphor perhaps for her skills at covering up unpleasantness, hiding her feelings from others and keeping secrets. She is the repository in the novel for all the hidden stories that no-one wants the general public to find out: Brandon's two Elizabeths, Lucy Steele and Edward's engagement, her sister's predicament and Willoughby's confession.

As the Dashwood sisters make their choices of marriage partner, there are many other such partnerships around them for them to be guided by. Their own mother was a second choice (like both Marianne and Elinor) and, while her marriage was a happy one, she was left almost destitute in favour of a male heir despite her years of attendance on her uncle-in-law. Another example of married bliss is John and Fanny Dashwood, the girls' half-brother and his wife, who, in a stunning few lines, talk themselves out of John's promise to his dying father. The marriages that the sisters encounter in Devonshire offer little better by way of example. The Middleton's sociability is brought about by a lack of any common interests between them; they seek company to distract themselves from one another and with the Palmers there is a wife who is continually finding amusement where none exists and a husband who is abusive and insulting:

> Charlotte laughed heartily to think her husband could not get rid of her; and exultingly said, she did not care how cross he was with her, as they must live together. It was impossible for anyone to be more thoroughly good natured, or more determined to be happy than Mrs Palmer. The studied

indifference, insolence and discontent of her husband gave her no pain: and when he scolded or abused her, she was highly diverted.

(Vol. I, Ch. 20)

There is also the example, narrated by Colonel Brandon, of an arranged marriage between his brother and their cousin Eliza and its tragic consequences. As well as this, there is the marriage of Lucy and Robert Ferrars, whose future we can imagine without being told, and the loveless marriage of Willoughby to the evil perpetrator of his letter to Marianne.

Given these examples, how well do the Dashwood sisters make their marriages? Edward rarely displays any attractive qualities and it is often easy to agree with Marianne's opinion of him as a poor lover. Elinor will be marrying into horrific in-laws and she is her husband's second choice. As for Marianne's final choice, much as Colonel Brandon loves her he says himself it is because she reminds him of another woman; she too is a second choice. And what does the vibrant Marianne give up in order to make a second attachment (which she professes is impossible) to the older man who wears flannel waistcoats? The novel's resolution assures us that Marianne "could never love by halves and her whole heart became, in time, as much devoted to her husband as it had once been to Willoughby." Marianne, whose eyes once sparkled now sees the world through different, more sober eyes. After her sickness she apologises to Elinor for the hurt and inconsiderateness she has shown to others. It is as if her sickness has restored her to respectable society. Clarity of vision has its consequences in loss of vigour and there is a certain abruptness in the way she is disposed of by her creator. Could all that passion really be harnessed into a dutiful and obedient wife, and if it is, would Brandon, the most passionate man in all of Austen's writing, the man who almost eloped with his cousin, fought a duel and looked after a ruined love child, still love her?

In many ways who Marianne marries is less significant than her change of heart. Throughout the novel we see her indulge her feelings, ignoring social mores and, as when she rides out with Willoughby, accepts the horse, visits his future home and accosts him in public, refuses to follow the conventional rules of her society. Even though she finds Lady Middleton and Mrs Jennings objectionable, she grabs at the chance of accompanying them to London. When things do go wrong for her, she collapses into an introspective state and even when she discovers her sister's unhappiness in the engagement of Edward to Lucy Steele it only leads her to more introspection, blaming herself for not noticing Elinor's pain. Her self-absorbing passions result in the fever and near death and when she recovers the passion is gone and it is her sister to whom she explains herself. The story has really ended when Elinor's cautious respect for society and its mores is vindicated and she who has patiently borne all the secrets and lies is rewarded with the deferential, but comparatively poor, Edward.

The theme of bad parenting and its consequences is written large in this novel and with a particular emphasis on the role of mothers. Lady Middleton over-indulges her children and credulously accepts the Steele sisters because of their fawning over them, Mrs Palmer becomes hysterical when her baby is in the same house as the feverish Marianne, the widowed Mrs Ferrars attempts to control the lives and marriages of her sons, doing enormous damage as a result, and Fanny Dashwood thrusts her infant son at his grandfather to win the inheritance, denying her half-sisters-in-law any charity in his name.

Sense and Sensibility also portrays the struggle between prosperity and propriety. The story turns around two great properties, Norland and Barton, and the people who live off the incomes from them. There is also Cleveland, owned by another upper-class man, Mr Palmer, soon to be an MP, and the smaller Delaford, owned by Colonel Brandon and badly run down by a profligate former owner but which the colonel's good sense of propriety, in its old-fashioned usage, is bringing back to prosperity. Willoughby stands to inherit the Allenham estate, smaller again than Delaford but still a fortune when added to his own estate at Combe Magna. All these men and the two wealthy widows, Mrs Jennings and Mrs Ferrars, live on income from their estates and investments. Few ever talk about, or are seen to manage, their estates, or do anything but enjoy themselves. The exceptions to this are Colonel Brandon who has brought his brother's ruined estate back to health, and John Dashwood, whose improvements – buying up neighbouring properties, enclosing the common land that the peasants would have relied on for their animals to feed, cutting down ancient walnut trees to make way for greenhouses – are all antisocial and self seeking. The characters in this story are regulated and controlled by the whims of a few wealthy people – the Middletons, John and Fanny Dashwood, Mrs Ferrars, Mrs Jennings and Lady Middleton – and no one here works. Those who are privileged by wealth either fail in their duty of concern for those in their power or indiscriminately use their money for their own entertainment, allowing others to benefit indiscriminately. In *Mansfield Park* and in *Northanger Abbey*, by way of comparison, there is much emphasis on the work that goes into running an estate well.

At the mercy of these wealthy people are most of the other characters in the novel, principally the Dashwood sisters and their mother. While Mrs Dashwood's income does not render them poor in any sense that the lower classes would understand, it is comparatively small. Edward Ferrars has a tiny income from an inheritance but it is insufficient to maintain the lifestyle to which he aspires. His brother is not dissimilar, and then there are the Steele sisters, whose lives consist of ingratiating themselves with rich people in order to get about in society and meet husbands. Finally, there is Willoughby, who must marry for money because he has wasted his own.

An important marker of wealth, and consequently freedom from constraint, is the ability to keep a carriage. Those who could are entirely independent of others while those who cannot, like the Miss Steeles and Miss Dashwoods, are utterly dependent on others. Willoughby's offer of a horse would give Marianne a freedom of movement proscribed to young, poor gentry of her kind. As Mrs Jennings mentions, it is Willoughby's insistence on keeping a horse and carriage which has put him in such dire straits that he must marry Miss Grey.

There is much talk about wealth in this novel. The sisters discuss what would make an acceptable income, with Elinor's aspirations more modest than her sister's, and Mrs Jennings talks constantly of the prospects of the various husbands-to-be and the value of the wives they are choosing. Women have value from the inheritance they bring, the rank of the family that they come from and their beauty. When Marianne grows sick, Mrs Jennings is concerned that her ability to catch a rich husband has dropped with her loss of bloom.

The end of the novel, like all the others, is a series of marriages for its young people, many of them in this case deeply unsatisfactory. But the marriages are less important than the learning process and in this novel the learning seems at times overdone, a clinical lesson rather than an emotional and cognitive one. Since Austen's novels are about how the heroine learns a sense of propriety, what do the Dashwood sisters learn? Marianne clearly comes to a clarity of vision, recognising the emotional harm she has done, chiefly to herself by her self-absorption, her overwrought sensibility. But is there not a sense of loss in Marianne's learning experience? She will certainly be a good wife, and benefit from understanding how to erect screens between her feelings and those who could harm them, but in order to gain good sense Marianne has lost her affective strength, her capacity to love ecstatically and totally. There is much that is attractive in the scenes between Marianne and Willoughby and we are right there with her when she accosts him in public. Her directness and vision sort out her confused relations with Willoughby once and for all, whereas Elinor's secrets and suppression of feelings drag out her own and Edward's unhappiness for half the novel. We can imagine Marianne, after being told Elinor's secret, fronting up to Edward and asking him what on earth was going on anyway. In the larger scale of things, what impropriety was there in Marianne's conduct with Willoughby? A few people gossiped about her but did she hurt anyone except herself?

What does Elinor learn? Her sense of propriety has helped a conniving little gold-digger to almost ruin the life of the man she herself loves. She has kept secrets from those who could help her in her own misery, and she comes to marry and have a means of living by a series of accidents rather than through her own learning process. Passion is seen to be more destructive than laudable or liberating, and only repression and secrecy can protect one from those excessively polite but malignant forces that 'good' society nurtures. It is a grim kind of lesson to learn about life and one that goes a long way to undermine any simple opposition between sense and sensibility.

3

Pride and Prejudice

Pride and Prejudice was written in its earliest form in 1796-7, after the epistolary novel which later became *Sense and Sensibility*. It was her first complete novel and the third to be submitted to a publisher, Thomas Cadell, who must have come to bitterly regret his reluctance to publish them. It sat on a shelf, read only by her friends for 15 years until, after her success with the rewritten *Sense and Sensibility*, it was "lop't and crop't" as Miss Austen put it and submitted to Thomas Egerton, who took it, copyright and all, for £110.

While *Sense and Sensibility* may be read as a debate between romanticism and good sense, *Pride and Prejudice* examines the human ability to make judgements and to revise them. The novel's heroine prides herself on her quick understanding and judgement of situations. She spots Mr Collins for a fool before she even meets him, knows Bingley's sisters are snobs, discerns the nature of Lady Catherine de Bourgh after one meeting and approves of the simple-minded but genuine Bingley. She fails horribly, of course, in other areas where she must make judgements. She mistakes Darcy, Wickham, her own best friend, Charlotte, her own father and above all, for most of the novel, she mistakes her own feelings. The novel's original title, *First Impressions*, (it was changed after another novel of the same title was published) gives us a stronger clue as to Austen's concerns and much of the fun of the novel for the reader is in knowing full well both Darcy's feelings, a rare occasion when the author allows us to know the feelings of one of her heroes, and Elizabeth's long before she knows them herself. What Elizabeth learns in this novel is to distinguish between first impressions and real understanding, opinion and knowledge.

Like the Dashwood sisters, Elizabeth and her sisters have little going for them in the marriage stakes. The two eldest have grace and beauty, qualities that are worth quite a good match but not in themselves a guarantee of success in the matrimonial marketplace, but the other daughters are fairly hopeless although, unlike the Dashwoods whose father's uncle had a choice in making his will and chose to ignore their needs, their poor prospects are the result of no one's judgement. Their father's estate is entailed to the next male heir. There is no one to blame here, no railing against the injustices of society, except of course by Mrs Bennet, and so the whole story begins on a much lighter note.

The community these girls and their neighbours inhabit is a socially narrow one, where Mr Bennet can comment with a degree of bitterness: "For what do we live but to make sport for our neighbours and laugh at them in our turn." (Vol. III, Ch. 15) Composed chiefly of a very small number of families, very little changes, neighbours know everyone's business and, as the opening lines indirectly inform us, an entire society lives by mistaking first impressions for genuine perception:

> It is a truth universally acknowledged that a single man in possession of a good fortune must be in want of a wife.

The sensitive and witty Elizabeth is surrounded by snobbery and crassness and has only her angelic sister, who refuses to believe ill of anyone, and her cynical, withdrawn father to share her ideas with. Her mother is a fool, her sisters badly brought up, her best friend takes a dolt for a husband in the sure knowledge of what she is doing, and her aunt is a well-meaning but silly gossip.

Into this small world sudden changes are brought about as the militia, a temporary military force created by fear of a French invasion, is billeted on the neighbourhood. With the addition of a wealthy young man and his family and friend, the tiny community's horizons are suddenly expanded far beyond the small social round of everyday life.

One of the most obvious aspects of *Pride and Prejudice*, elevating it beyond the reach of contemporary novels, is its leading lady, Elizabeth. Unlike the traditional heroine, Elizabeth is discerning, has a fine sense of irony and is a little bitter at life while still enjoying its ridiculousness:

> There are few people whom I really love, and still fewer of whom I think well. The more I see of the world, the more I am dissatisfied with it; and every day confirms my belief in the inconsistency of all human characters, and of the little dependence that can be placed on the appearance of either merit or sense.
>
> (Vol. II, Ch. 1)

One suspects that this sentence was not part of the early *First Impressions* and that it was added by a later, more mature Austen, a woman who was by then in her thirties.

Elizabeth shares with her father the fine but essentially defensive sense of irony that has him withdraw to his study and his books but puts her out there at the balls and gatherings in search of a possible husband and at the mercy of the people of whom she despairs. She observes all the proprieties proper to the roles in life of a young girl who, depending on her company, is a sister, daughter, neighbour or friend. At the same time, though, she knows her own sense of worth and this remains more important to her sense of identity and well being. In this respect, given that the predominating social mores of the time determined women's behaviour and life choices, Elizabeth is a kind of female fantasy figure. Elizabeth aspires to be, and is expected to become, someone's wife and, like Charlotte, she is seriously constrained by her lack of fortune; if she is not to live out her life in useless, genteel poverty, she must find a husband. She refuses to accept this imperative and will only marry if her conscience tells her that she can accept a proposal which is morally sound. Elizabeth strikes a note of female autonomy, demanding to be taken seriously as a rational thinker and not a female defined by her dependency on others. Her future choices will be made regardless of class, wealth and gender. Her marriage to Darcy cuts across all these things. She challenges the roles expected of her, which itself has a degree of fantasy to it, and yet still manages to find the perfect marriage.

Elizabeth, by means of her wit and liveliness, challenges the roles she must play. Like her father, she often stands outside her social roles and laughs at them and this is what she does when dancing at Netherfield with Darcy. She challenges him to talk to her by mocking the social roles that they should both be undertaking, just as Henry

Tilney does in *Northanger Abbey*. Earlier, her journey across muddy fields to Netherfield to visit her sister is a violation of many rules of decorum for nicely brought up young ladies but it suits her needs. It is important to point out, however, that Elizabeth challenges these rules but never flaunts them altogether. In this important respect, there is a fine distinction between her and her sister; Lydia is wild, Elizabeth is lively.

Part of Elizabeth's pride, and this is also part of her attractiveness to Darcy, lies in this liveliness and independence of spirit. She is aware of the roles that people have to play to fit in to society but she is willing to occasionally move out of those roles in pursuance of honesty. She knows she has no fortune but will only speak and act from her heart and is willing and happy to flaunt convention to do so. It is this individuality and strength of character that seems to set Bingley's sisters against her. Faced with Elizabeth's humour and unconventionality, their limited understanding and snobbery are threatened.

In sharp contrast to the quickwitted Elizabeth is her sister Jane, who carries out her social roles so well and with such simple sincerity that we forgive her for her naivety. She is so pleasant and willing to believe the best of people that she never makes any critical judgements at all, seeing the best in all people and, when confronted with the need to admit that either Mr Darcy or Mr Wickham is bad, chooses to see Wickham's story of his ill-treatment by Darcy as a misunderstanding between them. It is, though, only Jane's apparent simplicity and openness of mind which allows Mr Darcy to be anything other than proud and haughty.

Despite her finely-tuned ability to judge others, Elizabeth sometimes fails to make a correct judgement at important moments and so she misses that spark that flies between herself and Darcy at the assembly. His overheard slighting of herself touches on her vanity and her social self-consciousness, blinding her from being more critically aware of his possible attraction towards her. Consequently, in their following meetings, she misreads his clearly romantic interest in her, considering his study of her as another slight and telling herself that she does not care. But it is exactly her reactions to his unwanted and misunderstood attention, expressed as they are in her strong opinions, her debunking of social clichés and her refusal to acquiesce and flatter, that attract him. At some level, Elizabeth Bennet half knows this when she parades around the room with Miss Bingley:

> Elizabeth, having rather expected to affront him, was amazed at his gallantry; but there was a mixture of sweetness and archness in her manner which made it difficult for her to affront anybody; and Darcy had never been so bewitched by any woman as he was by her.
>
> (Vol. I, Ch. 10)

Elizabeth makes a second serious failure in judgement when she meets the attractive, chatty, plausible Mr Wickham. Immediately on meeting him, instead of wondering about the motives of a complete stranger so readily revealing private matters, she accepts his story about Darcy's ill-treatment. The reader has to ask why this discerning, bright young woman does not notice the attraction she holds for Darcy, misreading his reserved nature for standoffishness, while promptly accepting the friendship of another man and flirting a little with the idea of a romance with him. Her sensible aunt Gardiner has already warned her about Wickham but a part of her blocks this out of her consciousness. Perhaps, as Andrew H. Wright suggests in *Jane Austen's Novels: A Study in Structure*, an explanation for her mistake is to be found in her strong, bright personality. Wickham never really means that much to her and she can flirt and talk and dance with him and never become entangled, never make an emotional commitment. Perhaps she recognises in Darcy the strength of feelings that might be involved if she ever considered her own feelings in that direction. Bright, independent Elizabeth, who can laugh at anybody, could be badly hurt by this complex man; the shallow, shiny Wickham has no layers at all to get lost in.

Mr Collins' proposal is both hilarious and serious. Here we see what Elizabeth is up against – the overbearing belief of a male that a woman is just an elegant female, using tricks to catch her man. Elizabeth, crying out in distress that this is not so, calls to mind a passage that Austen may have read in Mary Wollstonecraft's *Rights of Women*: "Do not consider me now as an elegant female intending to plague you, but as a rational creature speaking truth from the heart." Mr Collins' refusal to countenance her rejection stems also from his sure belief that since she has no dowry no other man could possibly want her. This is the social context missing from the epigram of the opening lines, the perspective that makes it seem more to be a truth universally acknowledged that a woman with no dowry must be in want of a husband.

The start of the learning experience which Elizabeth undergoes comes about as a result of this comic encounter with Mr Collins. For most of her 21 years she has lived in a state of confidence in her own discernment, choosing, as she sees it, her friends with care and thinking she knows them well. She is genuinely astonished when her good friend Charlotte agrees to marry Mr Collins, a man she cannot possibly have any respect for, out of sheer material need. Yet prior to this, Charlotte has told Elizabeth quite plainly her ideas about marriage and one's chances of happiness in it. Elizabeth has plainly heard her friend's quite simple belief that it is important to secure a marriage first and worry about happiness afterwards but she failed to understand that Charlotte would indeed make important life choices on the basis of these beliefs. In this sense, Elizabeth did not know her good friend as well as she thought she did. She does not, however, manage to extrapolate from this misjudgement the idea that she may be making other misjudgements of character.

From the chaotic home of Longbourne, where her father openly ridicules his wife, and from an aunt who encourages her nieces to flirt with the militia billeted on the town of Meryton, Elizabeth moves to the socially superior ambiance of Rosings. What she encounters is a stifling atmosphere and a parsonage house where the occupants defer in all their doings to the great lady. Here Elizabeth and Darcy reconvene their dialogue and she half suspects by this time that it was he who consciously separated Jane and Bingley and put a stop to their happiness. After a few more scenes of his paying attention, and her apparent failure to realise that he is attracted to her, the wonderful scene takes place where Darcy lays out for Elizabeth all her family's shortcomings in the most abrupt and selfish way possible and Elizabeth has the presence of mind to put him in his place.

Darcy's proposal mirrors Mr Collins', both assume that any unpropertied young woman must accept with gratitude any offer of marriage in whatever terms it is made – "In vain have I struggled," says Darcy, with more honesty than tact.

Here, at the heart of the novel, the learning process which all Austen's heroines undergo is well in hand. Elizabeth has prided herself on her judgement, wit and unconventionality and has failed miserably to see her family, particularly her father, as others must see them. Her interview with Darcy and then his letter are learning experiences for her, making her see clearly what an unattractive family she has. She comes to recognise that her sister's mild manners have led Darcy to believe that there was no real attachment. Her poor judgement of Wickham falls into place as she examines his behaviour in the light of Darcy's letter and she exclaims: "How despicably have I acted ... I who have prided myself on my discernment! I who have valued myself on my abilities! Who have often disdained the generous candour of my sister, and gratified my vanity in useless or blameable distrust. How humiliating is this discovery ... Had I been in love, I could not have been more wretchedly blind." Her final exclamation shows what more learning she has to go through. She does not yet know her own feelings.

Houses play an important role in the landscape of an Austen novel and nowhere is this more apparent than when Elizabeth moves from her own entailed and contentious household, first to the ornate and stultifying Rosings and then to Pemberly. At first sight Elizabeth becomes aware of the honour Darcy has bestowed upon her: "To be mistress of Pemberly might be something." Unlike the heroines of the other novels of Austen's time, who encounter dark, dangerous houses with secrets locked up in them, Elizabeth finds rooms "lofty and handsome, and their furniture suitable to the fortune of their proprietor ... neither gaudy nor uselessly fine; with less of splendour and more of real elegance than the furniture of Rosings". Here everything, even the view, is open and fine. The feelings she first had after reading Darcy's letter begin to coalesce after the praise of his housekeeper. She stands in the heart of his house, the place where he is most natural and well known, and looks up at his portrait:

> What praise is more important than the praise of an intelligent servant? As a brother ... landlord ... master she considered how many people's happiness were in his guardianship! ... and as she stood before the canvas on which he was represented, and fixed his eyes upon herself, she thought of his regard with a deeper sentiment of gratitude than it had ever raised before.
>
> (Vol. III, Ch. 1)

The heroine's learning process is nearly completed after the praise from his housekeeper and his kindness to her more respectable Aunt and Uncle Gardiner. Darcy has clearly learned the difference between first impressions and fact also. After his attentions to her family there we hear:

> She respected, she esteemed, she was grateful to him, she felt a real interest in his welfare; and she only wanted to know how far she wished that welfare to depend upon herself, and how far it should be for the happiness of both that she should employ the power, which her fancy told her she still possessed, of bringing on the renewal of his addresses.
>
> (Vol. III, Ch. 2)

Elizabeth still has not quite completed her learning experience. The reader can almost hear Elizabeth approaching the word 'love' but, choosing instead terms like respect, esteem, grateful, turning away from it with the use of a less intensive vocabulary.

In terms of Elizabeth's learning process, the rest of the novel – the elopement and the interview with Lady Catherine – is a bit of melodrama designed to have Elizabeth finally realise, when all hope is gone, when her family has put itself beyond the point where any self-respecting man could think of attaching himself to it, that Darcy was the man for her:

> She began now to comprehend that he was exactly the man, who, in disposition and talents, would most suit her. His understanding and temper, though unlike her own, would have answered all her wishes. It was an union that must have been to the advantage of both; by her ease and liveliness, his mind might have been softened, his manners improved, and from his judgement, information and knowledge of the world she must have received benefit of great importance.
>
> (Vol. III, Ch. 8)

All that is left, then, is for Lady Catherine to step in and close the deal for them. Elizabeth's refusal to deny her relationship with Darcy gives him hope, the two pairs of lovers are reunited and in a few brief paragraphs all the characters in the book are tidied away: Mary becomes her mother's companion, Mrs Bennet remains exactly the same, Mr Bennet enjoys making visits to Pemberly, Kitty learns from her two eldest sisters how to be a better person and Lydia and Wickham carry on unrepentant, scrounging cash from the sisters whenever they can.

Moving beyond the love story, the society of Meryton is also subjected to the kind of criticism that formed the basis for Elizabeth's self-education. It is a society that makes hasty judgements, swayed into expressions of certainty by opinion, self-delusion and insufficient evidence. In Meryton, which believes any young man of independent fortune to be in need of a wife, any new person or piece of news is common property. Wickham turns up in Meryton having been persuaded by Denny on a whim to join the militia and his pleasing appearance and natural ways make him an instant favourite. His story of mistreatment immediately becomes fact, until the news of his elopement hits the town when suddenly the 'truth' changes:

> All Meryton seemed to be striving to blacken the man, who, but three months before had been almost an angel of light. He was declared to be in debt to every tradesman in the place, and his intrigues, all honoured with the title of seduction, had been extended into every tradesman's family.
> (Vol. III, Ch. 6)

Similarly, Darcy's character was instantly determined by the gentle folk of Meryton: "His character was decided. He was the proudest, most disagreeable man in the world and everybody hoped he would never come there again." (Vol. I, Ch. 3)

When the news of first Lydia's elopement and then Jane's engagement finds its way to the village, "The Bennets were speedily pronounced to be the luckiest family in the world though only a few weeks before when Lydia had first run away, they had generally been proved to be marked out for misfortune." (Vol. III, Ch. 14) This is a community where first impressions are taken for facts. The error in judgement extends far beyond the simple folk of Meryton. Mrs Gardiner is guilty of taking impression for fact also, as she does when she thinks she remembers hearing that Mr Darcy was proud as a child.

Much of the humour of the novel emerges from the unusual intermixing of rounded, psychologically believable characters with the equally sharply drawn but greatly exaggerated caricatures. Mrs Bennet, Lady Catherine, Mr Collins and Lydia are, despite their presence as caricatures, far more memorable people than, say, Jane or Charlotte. Perhaps this is because they are all horrible reminders of aspects of people that we may have encountered. Lady Catherine believes entirely in her role in society to the point where she feels she can decide on the next day's weather, ask impertinent questions or plan the lives of those around her. She has no awareness of the effect she has on those around her. Lydia, too, lacks attractiveness because she is too consumed by her social role play. Her mother has taught her to find a husband and she has, at the expense of developing an inner, reflective life and with the consequence that she never contemplates the hurt she has caused. Mr Collins is not dissimilar in this respect, his pomposity and almost grovelling politeness being a function of his unreflective and very stupid view of the duties and rights of a clergyman and client of Lady Catherine. The highlights of the novel, the points where we feel something has been achieved, are not in the later somewhat coy conversations between Darcy and Elizabeth but in these great flaming encounters – Mr Collins' comic proposal crashing into Elizabeth's attempts at reason and her refusal to play her role of grateful, penniless spinster, Lady Catherine's visit to Longbourne where again Elizabeth refuses to take on the role of minion, Lydia's arrival home with her new husband, the moment when Elizabeth tells her mother she is engaged to Mr Darcy. The comical figures in these encounters, like the Bingley sisters and the Lucases, are incapable of change, of learning the differences between surface and depth. It is precisely this ability or willingness to learn that makes Elizabeth, and to a lesser extent Darcy, different and more admirable individuals.

A peripheral but still interesting figure in this novel is Mary, whose future is to be a companion to her mother while her other sister Kitty joins Elizabeth and Jane in their more cultured society. What exactly has this girl done to deserve such a fate? If Elizabeth cries out to be considered a rational woman, Mary has taken on the social role of rationality with none of the understanding that goes with it. She has application but no talent and is every bit as proud of herself as Mr Collins. It is a shame the two did not get together. At one stage Mr Collins is called on to read aloud to the family and chooses James

Fordyce's *Sermons to Young Women* (1766), a book of conduct which equates women who read novels with prostitutes. Such books dictating good conduct to young women were very popular and much of Mary's philosophy seems to derive from them: "loss of virtue in a female is irretrievable ... one false step involves her in endless ruin ... her reputation is no less brittle than it is beautiful." Mary has only empty epigrams to fall back on because she lacks the emotions or empathy that could be brought to a situation. In fact, all her epigrams are proved false as Lydia does not experience the endless ruin Mary prophesies.

Mr Bennet holds a special place in this novel. In the early chapters he emerges as a kind of commentator on Meryton society, laughing at his wife and at social customs even as he reluctantly takes part in them. Mrs Bennet, Mr Collins, his silly daughters are all the more amusing for his sardonic commentary on their shallow, one-note performances. Like Elizabeth he is a complex character, delighting in words and the foolish uses that people put them to. He provides a foil and an ally for Elizabeth, drawing her into his witty observances on society, and we realise that her humour is much like his must have been before the disappointment of his marriage. As the story unfolds, though, the drawbacks to his wit are discovered, first as he publicly humiliates Mary, then as his younger daughters grow wilder in their behaviour unchecked by him. He alone is Elizabeth's equal in intelligence for while Darcy is educated and noble he displays no flashing wit or depth of understanding. It is only with Mr Bennet that Elizabeth reveals her serious side, when she begs him to stop Lydia going to Brighton with the Forsters, and it is only with him that she seriously talks about her love for Darcy. He is a sad figure, telling Elizabeth: "My child, let me not have the grief of seeing *you* unable to respect your partner in life." The emphasis on *you* suggests that he is thinking of his own marriage. Briefly he admits his responsibility for Lydia's behaviour: "You may well warn me against such an evil. Human nature is so prone to fall into it! No, Lizzy, let me once in my life feel how much I have been to blame. I am not afraid of being overpowered by the impression. It will pass away soon enough." And so it does and he returns to his sardonic humour, pretending to value Wickham above all his new sons-in-law, revelling in the stupidity of Mr Collins' letter. His humour is defensive – a way of protecting himself against all the fools he has to deal with and the consequences of a foolish marriage.

Ultimately, though, like the other citizens of Meryton, Mr Bennet learns nothing. He learned all he needed long ago when his pretty, lively wife turned out to be a shrill, mindless fool. He remains an isolated figure, passing every bit as sarcastic comments as he ever did on his daughters' marriages and husbands and delighting in making surprise visits to Pemberly.

Darcy, it has been noted by critics, is a mere shadow of a man, far less clearly drawn than Wickham. We are told he is Elizabeth's perfect mate and his actions show that he really wants her for his wife. He, like Elizabeth, recognises that theirs will be a beneficial partnership. But he is essentially a remote figure. In Volume I he stands aloof from Meryton but also from the fawning Caroline Bingley. He seems proud to say, "My good opinion once lost is lost for ever", or to comment that Elizabeth is tolerable but not enough to tempt him to dance. His proposal to Elizabeth is haughty and proud and insulting. It is at Pemberly that he becomes an attractive figure, both to the reader and to Elizabeth. He becomes a good landlord and master through the report of his housekeeper. His later heroic actions are reported to us and Elizabeth in a letter and his return to Longbourne is marked with more silence. The few intimate conversations with Elizabeth reveal little more about him, and even Elizabeth cannot look at him during his second proposal. But he is humbled, and ready to accept the evil Wickham and still worse, Mrs Bennet, as his relations.

Is there any sense in which Elizabeth finds Darcy sexually attractive? Do we sense that Lydia has run off with Wickham because of a burning, passionate desire for him? There is very little physical contact in *Pride and Prejudice* but there are glances, blushes, haughty expressions and arch looks, even a dirty petticoat. The lives of these characters are carried out in public spaces – drawing rooms, assembly halls, country lanes – and there is very little opportunity for closeness. Elizabeth and Darcy's love affair is one of looks and language rather than physical proximity. Both are described in their visible, social parts, their eyes, faces and dress and their courtship takes place in formal dances where the two at most brush hands as they stand and move in patterns, exchanging conversation as they come together and falling silent as they part. Their talk is all about conduct, character, prudence. Similarly, Lydia's elopement is all about excitement and fun, rather than sex, and her passion is rewarded by being permanently attached to a cad. Besides Lydia, Mr Bennet is one of the few characters in the novel whose passion allows him to fall for a pretty face and the consequence of that was a unfulfilling marriage. When Elizabeth comes to realise that she loves Darcy and could make him a good wife, it is the material reality she thinks about rather than the physical attractions of the man, his power and influence and her wit and liveliness.

Letters play an important part in this novel and it is possible that the first drafts of *First Impressions* took the form of an epistolary novel. Although the final version benefits from flashing repartee and comic conversations, the piece of writing which sits right at the heart of the novel is Darcy's letter to Elizabeth. The story thus far has been one of Elizabeth's impressions of first Darcy and then Wickham and her response to Wickham's story. We have seen how humiliated she is by her family's behaviour and how much she loves a sister not given to outward shows of affection and a father who takes nothing seriously and laughs at everything, even his own family's behaviour. Darcy's letter completely rewrites the story, retelling the whole thing from a different perspective, allowing Elizabeth to change her judgement and readers to alter their perspective also. We have laughed with Mr Bennet up till now but we can finally see the harm he has done his family. A close comparison between Wickham's story and Darcy's reveals omissions on Wickham's part rather than downright lies and so we and Elizabeth are presented with a change in perspective rather than a different version of the truth. Earlier, Caroline Bingley's letters to Jane are given two interpretations, Jane's naïve one and Elizabeth's more astute interpretation.

The success of *Pride and Prejudice* as a popular story and material for television and film screenplays has more to do with it resembling a rather beautiful fairy story set in an imaginary town called Meryton than with the social reality that Austen was engaging with and bringing to life in the novel. Set in the closing years of the 18th century when the threat of a French invasion was very real, the story almost imperceptively draws a picture of social change. The Gardiners are in trade, their house is close beside their warehouses, and they live in an unfashionable part of London. Despite their associations with trade, they are genteel and courteous people. The Lucases, on the other hand, are also in trade but lack the understanding of the Gardiners. Their behaviour is all manners but with no appreciation of the nature of real courtesy. Beneath the Gardiners and the Phillips and the Lucases are the general tradespeople of the town, whose daughters are all at risk from males like Wickham, and beneath them again are the Bennets' servants. The Bennets have two housemaids, one is actually graced with a name and a line to say in the novel, and a manservant. Meryton, unlike Mansfield Park or Highbury, has no deserving poor for Elizabeth to take comfort in by way of bringing soup or clothing to, although perhaps Pemberly offers more rewarding prospects in this regard.

Mr Bingley represents new money. He has inherited a hundred thousand pounds, enormous wealth. He is from the north of England and his family's wealth has come from one of the new trades that underlay the Industrial Revolution. They are so newly rich that they have not had time to establish a landed estate, and Bingley is wandering about looking for one. To be really secure in their new social role, the Bingleys must marry old money and Caroline Bingley has hopes of doing just that. She plans to marry Darcy and her brother will marry Darcy's sister. Elizabeth and her sisters are members of the older, landed gentry but their wealth is deteriorating as her father, his estate entailed, lives off his income and fails to put any money by for harder times. Lady Catherine and Darcy are the real old money and Lady Catherine wishes to perpetuate their class position by marrying Darcy off to his cousin, whose sickliness seems symptomatic of a falling off in the solidity of their aristocratic status. Mr Darcy is one of a dying breed, a member of the ruling classes who fulfils his role as master and caretaker of a great estate and the people in it. Darcy looks down on Elizabeth's family for their crass behaviour and their association with the lower classes but he is able to form a rapprochement with the Gardiners. Although they come from a different social class, they share a common respect for others and a politeness of the heart which transcends class divisions. When Elizabeth marries Darcy she will take her rightful place among those people who in Austen's view regulate and keep order in a simple, courtesy-led, rural society. It is fitting that Darcy should meet the

Gardiners in his estate, carefully tended but not to the point of artificiality, on a bridge, a place where two sides meet. *Pride and Prejudice* is Jane Austen's comic fantasy of the rejuvenation of an old way of life, the energy and vitality of a girl, not too unlike herself, being grafted into the class which determines and regulates the society that she sees fast fading away around her.

4

Mansfield Park

From the romantic to the morally sublime, the change in tone from *Pride and Prejudice* to *Mansfield Park* could not be any sharper. By 1809, Jane Austen's father was dead and her wealthy brother had provided the comfortably large cottage at Chawton for Jane, now aged 34 and a confirmed spinster, her sister Cassandra, their mother and another female relative. At Chawton, Jane found the time and the peace of mind to write again after a long period of change and an unsettled life. Within two years she was writing *Mansfield Park* and in 1814, in the final year of the Napoleonic Wars, this new work by Austen, by now a popular published writer, was available to the public.

Mansfield Park, Austen's most complex work, shifts readers' attention to a darker, less easily resolved plane than is to be found in any of her earlier novels. Its complexity lies in Austen's creation of psychologically believable characters within a story that focuses attention on areas of concern beyond just the family. Her new novel was decidedly new in the way it examines the state of the nation.

The result is a complex work of fiction that invites a range of interpretation. Reading the novel from a conservative, traditionally Austenian perspective, *Mansfield Park* is the author's cry from the heart for the older ways that Britain was losing. *Mansfield Park*, especially for the period when Sir Thomas goes away and Tom Bertram takes charge of the house, represents the nation at the end of a lifetime of war with France, with a dandy, profligate regent ruling in place of a mad king. Ultimately, though, Sir Thomas Bertram learns from the outsider, Fanny, what real values are, and a reduced family circle is strengthened by the trials which its own mismanagement created in the first place. A happy ending, just. A very different point of view, while still seeing *Mansfield Park* as a emblem for the nation, points to how the grand house and estates of Sir Thomas Bertram depend for their existence on the capitalist enterprise of the slave trade and Britain's imperial greed. Sir Thomas' management of his property is corrupted by his need to be absent while administering his foreign income and, within the terms of this radically different moral universe, the unfolding of the plot enacts a form of nemesis. The novel ends with Tom Bertram still in a sickly state and the family surrounded by morally hollow freebooters like the Crawfords. The final plight of the Bertrams is one of withdrawal and a failure to forgive those who have sinned against it.

The complexity of *Mansfield Park* is that the novel can sustain both of these interpretations. Attempts by some critics to try and establish what Austen 'really' meant do not provide a way of adjudicating between the radically different ways of reading the novel. Research into her letters, accounts of what she was reading at the time and what her political opinions may have been are not conclusive and, indeed, may be beside the point.

The richness of *Mansfield Park* is its ability to sustain different interpretations and this applies to questions of characterization as well as broader questions about the 'meaning' of the novel as a whole. Is Fanny a pain in the backside and a prig or a saintly upholder of all that is valuable, and if she is both is this good or bad? Does Fanny's sister, Susan, become a mere commodity to be purchased by the Bertrams or is she released from a degrading home life with few expectations? Is Maria a nasty wrongdoer who deserves to be cast out or is she the victim of a society which places connections and wealth above happiness? If Crawford had married Fanny might he have become a better man? Other doubts may linger in the minds of readers. What are we to make of a marriage between first cousins and a father incapable of providing a moral code for his children?

The plot, briefly. Three sisters have made very different marriages. One marries Sir Thomas Bertram, the owner of Mansfield Park and sugar plantations in Antigua. Another marries Mr Norris, a clergyman who, through Sir Thomas, gets a living near to the Bertram estate. The third marries without prospects and is disowned by the two respectable sisters. In serious distress, the third sister applies to the other two for help and Mrs Norris arranges for one of the children to live at Mansfield Park. Timid and ignorant, little Fanny finds comfort there only in her cousin Edmund. She grows up in the shadow of the two confident Bertram girls, Julia and Maria, is physically weak and constantly reminded by her aunt Norris of her duty of gratitude for the family's charity.

Sir Thomas goes away for two years and in that time Maria becomes engaged to a wealthy but brainless young man, Mr Rushworth. The Crawfords, sister and brother, join the family's social group and matters become unhinged as Edmund begins to fall in love with Mary Crawford, Maria falls for the flirting Crawford and Julia gets the sulks because she wants Crawford too. Meanwhile, Mary Crawford learns that Edmund intends to become a clergyman. Two events, which will be looked at later, stand out in all of this: the visit to Sotherton Court, Mr Rushworth's home, and the amateur dramatics at Mansfield.

Sir Thomas returns, Maria marries Rushworth and Crawford decides first to break Fanny's heart and then that he will marry her. Fanny, however, refuses him and is sent to Portsmouth to think about her decision. Tom Bertram, Sir Thomas' heir, gets desperately ill and Maria runs off with Crawford, justifying all Fanny's objections, and Julia elopes with Mr Yates, another worthless young man. Fanny returns and becomes the centre of all that is good in the family. Mary Crawford displays her immorality by suggesting that the affair be all hushed up and Edmund, now a clergyman, abandons all hope of her. After an unspecified time the cousins Edmund and Fanny marry.

One way of considering how we should understand all of this is by way of Austen's style. In *Pride and Prejudice* her style varies through conversational dramatic scenes, interjections on the part of the narrator and letters expressing feelings by various characters. The reader's predominant means of experiencing the story, though, is through the mind of Elizabeth, aided by occasional trips into the thoughts of Charlotte, Darcy and Mr Collins, translated for us into free indirect speech by the narrator. Much of the humour of *Pride and Prejudice* emerges from technique, as in the scene where Elizabeth considers her feelings for Darcy. ("She respected, she esteemed, she was grateful to him, she felt a real interest in his welfare.") We and the author are standing beyond the words going through Elizabeth's mind and laughing delightedly at her because we know the real truth. This kind of irony is almost totally absent in the writer's treatment of Fanny Price. What you read is what you get and Fanny's opinion seems for the most part to be laid out for us, with no irony intended. The free indirect speech in this novel is there, but Fanny's thoughts are treated with absolute seriousness. This lack of irony and the very sympathetic way Fanny is treated suggests that it is a mistake to think Austen wants her readers to detect any priggishness in Fanny.

In this novel we are also allowed into the thoughts of the other characters, particularly Mary Crawford's. Sometimes, within one paragraph there is a switch from one person's thoughts to another's and we have to be sharp to notice the switch. In these instances, the irony, the part where we and the author can stand back and realise that the thought processes of the character are wrong or deluded in some way, is often apparent.

The most interesting characters in the book, witty, lively and talented, are the Crawfords. They are both very social creatures who know how to flatter and amuse their acquaintances. The two are orphans, displaced at an early age to the home of an aunt and uncle, Admiral and Mrs Crawford. Henry and Mary have both inherited fortunes and were spoiled by their new parents:

> Admiral and Mrs Crawford, though agreeing in nothing else, were united in affection for these children, or, at least, were no farther adverse in their feelings than that each had their favourite, to whom they showed the greatest fondness of the two. The Admiral delighted in the boy, Mrs Crawford doted on the girl; and it was the lady's death which now obliged her *protégée,* after some months' further trial at her uncle's house, to find another home. Admiral Crawford was a man of vicious conduct, who chose, instead of retaining his niece, to bring his mistress under his own roof ...
>
> (Vol. I, Ch. 4)

Thus Mary Crawford joins her half-sister in the living at Mansfield and in the early chapters there are constant hints at the disturbing early life she must have led. Her life has led her to a kind of cynicism, especially regarding marriage, which she claims is often full of deception and disappointment: " ... it is of all transactions, the one in which people expect most from others, and are least honest themselves … What is this but a take in?" (Vol. I, Ch. 5)

When Mrs Grant suggests that those disappointed in marriage may turn to other consolations, finding comfort in other activities, Mary agrees, saying that when she is married she will do likewise and wishes that all her friends would do the same: "It would save me many a heart ache". The reader is left wondering what could her aunt have suffered so as to make this girl so cynical. Mrs Grant hopes that staying at Mansfield will make Mary less cynical. Listening to her conversation you have to sympathise with Mary, but having portrayed her in this sympathetic light Jane Austen adds: "The Crawfords, without wanting to be cured (of their attitude to marriage), were very willing to stay." We feel sorry for Mary but then we are told that she has no wish to change; she enjoys her cynical attitude.

Given her beauty and lively manner it is inevitable that Edmund should fall for her, although she first sets her sights on Tom. He, however, has no interest in her. As the plot progresses, we are given insights into Mary's thoughts, and witness her odd mixture of kindness, worldliness and bad taste. At dinner she laughs of "rears and vices", a crude sexual innuendo, and later in the same scene she talks disparagingly of her uncle and his improvements of a summer cottage, which offends Edmund's sense of propriety. Later, when everyone is pressing Fanny to take part in the theatricals, she puts a stop to the pressure out of sympathy for Fanny's feelings.

Mary's life contrasts with and parallels Fanny's. Both are displaced persons damaged in early life, the one by the disruption of her removal from everything she knew and the other by a corrupt guardian. But unlike Fanny, Mary has no appreciation of silence or stillness, and must always be doing something. Unlike Fanny's timid efforts at riding a horse, she is quickly master of the skill and she enjoys it so much that "she did not know how to leave off".

The reader, along with Edmund, and for a while Fanny as well, sympathises with Mary. The damage inflicted on her by a poor upbringing leads us to appreciate her gradual attraction to Edmund since he represents everything that she has already told her aunt she finds lacking in most marriages:

> Without his being a man of the world, or an elder brother, without any of the arts of flattery or the gaieties of small talk, he began to be agreeable to her … he was not pleasant by any

common rule, he talked no nonsense, he paid no compliments, his opinions were unbending, his attentions tranquil and simple. There was a charm, perhaps in his sincerity, his steadiness, his integrity which Miss Crawford might be equal to feel, though not equal to discuss with herself.

(Vol. I, Ch. 7)

Here again we are privy to the thoughts of Mary Crawford and become torn between recognising her obvious appreciation of Edmund's good qualities and our knowledge that he is already loved by another, one with whom we have even more sympathy and understanding.

Finally though, Mary's hollow nature reveals itself. She seeks to cover up her brother's sleazy affair with Maria; having no understanding of the damage it has caused to everyone, she is only concerned with their public reputation. Although she can appreciate and love a man like Edmund for his good qualities, she has no understanding of what makes him good or what is lacking in her own moral makeup. What Fanny has known all along is that Mary is without morals, a snake in the grass, and it seems to be no coincidence that Mary's instrument is the harp, the instrument of the sirens who lure men to their deaths.

Part of Mary's attraction is her sense of companionship and intimacy with her brother. The contrast here is with the Bertrams, whom we never see supporting one another or sharing their feelings and, who seem rather to compete with one another. So we have Julia and Maria competing over Crawford and Tom domineering and curt with Edmund. With the exception of Edmund, they all treat Fanny as a commodity. We respond at first to the gaiety in the Crawfords' attitudes to marriage and Henry's flirting, rather than see it as a moral shortcoming, but by the end of the theatricals it is clear to us, and to Fanny, that Henry Crawford has caused great harm. On Henry's return to Mansfield he, unaware of how well Fanny is armed against him, endeavours to make her fall in love with him and we hear the comfortable but shocking banter between Henry and Mary as she warns him not to hurt her friend too much.

Like Mary, Henry is another damaged creature. He has all the skills and confidence of a sophisticated city dweller and although he is the novel's villain we cannot help liking the man and asking 'what if' over his proposal of marriage to Fanny. Like Wickham, his attractiveness is deliberately created. If Fanny and Edmund are not attracted to this brother and sister how else is their steadfastness of purpose and morality to be tried? But to a careful observer such as Fanny his wickedness is clear. He flirts with an engaged woman as well as encouraging her sister, both at Sotherton and during the theatricals and then blithely rides off leaving both sisters disappointed in love. With no one else to flirt with he plans mischief against Fanny, seeing it only as a challenge to his flirting skills.

Henry is as surprised as Mary was over Edmund to find himself falling in love with the object of his attentions and here he too becomes attractive to us because he shows the discernment of recognising her value. We hear his thoughts on the value of Fanny as a wife and it is as much for her moral certainties as for her prettiness and ability to show affection.

> The gentleness, modesty and sweetness of her character ... her temper ... her affections ... her understanding ... such a steadiness and regularity of conduct, such a high notion of honour, and such an observance of decorum ... Her faith and integrity.
>
> (Vol. II, Ch. 12)

Henry foresees the life he will have if he marries such a woman and he can appreciate how it will be full of comforts and with a companion with whom he could share all his thoughts. He recognises the wrongness of his attempt to make her love him for fun. Henry is suddenly a reformed man. He arranges for Fanny's brother William to get a promotion and when Fanny repeatedly refuses to agree to marry him, actually sees himself as she has seen him and promises to show her he can be a different man. He proposes to go off to his own estate and show by absence and good behaviour, that he is serious in his intent.

When Henry visits Portsmouth, his behaviour is faultless and even Fanny begins to think that he might have seriously reformed. To their audience of readers, the feeling must be creeping in that this is an honest change of heart and that Fanny might make him a genuinely better person. Alas, his will fails him and he elopes with Maria. In her final summation of the events she has described, the author breaks down Henry Crawford's character for us and makes it clear that he might have become a better person under Fanny's influence. Instead, he chooses not to return to his estate, takes up with Maria and hopes to keep the liaison a secret from Fanny. Henry Crawford is hollow at the core, he has no morals or values which, in the absence of Fanny's influence, can keep him behaving well. Crawford is a consummate actor. He becomes whatever person his whims determine and for a time merely acted the part of a moral person.

And so to Fanny. Our previous heroines had much to recommend them for all their failings: Elizabeth's humour is set against her misjudgements; Catherine's monumental naivety is mitigated by her brightness and curiosity; Marianne's wild romanticism is attractive in itself and she learns to be more thoughtful. Fanny, on the other hand, comes with very few failings for us to empathise with and very little in the way of liveliness for us to be amused by. She arrives at Mansfield Park almost by accident, certainly with very little thought on the part of her relatives as to what would become of her. She is translocated into a huge house, whose very size frightens her, and finds herself among strong, confident cousins and a terrifying uncle. She is made to understand that she will never be as important as her cousins and that she must be grateful to the people who have taken her away from everything she has known. Her first attachment is to Edmund as a brother to replace the brother she has lost. But throughout all these tribulations, Fanny somehow learns respect for the values of the house which she has no claim on. She makes herself useful to her aunts, bears Mrs Norris' bullying and expects no equal treatment with her cousins. By her 18th year, she is shy and frail but, despite being surrounded by a somewhat dysfunctional family, she has acquired a strong sense of good behaviour and morality. Thus armed, she is able to watch the family as it crumbles, first through the absence of the father, then by means of the gently corrupting influence of the Crawfords.

Fanny bears all that is thrown at her. First there is the anguish of seeing Edmund slip away from her, unable to see Mary Crawford for her true self, and then there are the unpleasant attentions paid to her by Henry Crawford, followed by her uncle's anger at her for refusing him and, worst of all, even Edmund's attempts to persuade her she is wrong. The final blow comes when she returns to the

Portsmouth home she has missed for eight years, only to find it shabby, chaotic and crowded, a kind of hell where each person seeks only their own comfort and where by comparison Henry Crawford and Mansfield Park seem so much more attractive.

Just as she is at her lowest point, expecting to hear of Edmund's engagement to Miss Crawford, all is overturned by a series of events: Tom's sickness; Crawford's affair; followed by Julia's elopement. Vindicated at last, Fanny returns to her true home, finally valued as the true daughter of the house when she alone is shown to have the values that are so important to the future of the family.

Fanny is never a cheery bundle of fun who overcomes her adverse circumstances but the reader is drawn to her by the treatment dished out at the hands of Mrs Norris and her female cousins. Throughout the first half of the novel, she is silent, watchful, obedient, willing to be made use of and unresentful of her role in the family. By the second half of the novel, she is beginning to bloom both physically and mentally. She gains the confidence to express her opinions, has the courage to stand up for what she knows to be right against the distantly authoritarian figure of her uncle, actually gets angry with Henry Crawford, takes charge of a ruinous household at Portsmouth and imposes a little order on it and teaches her sister some calmness.

The scenes at Portsmouth are worth considering carefully. In Fanny's memory, the place was home and yet when she arrives it is nothing like what she now understands by that term. Her father is a selfish, coarse man who spends his days drinking and finding out the news, while her mother is a slattern who exerts no parental control over angry, selfish children. The house is small, dark and noisy, the walls are thin and everywhere there is noise and squabbling and dirt. The place she considered home stands in sharp physical and social contrast to the house she now realises to be her true abode. Like Austen's other heroines, Fanny has learned an important lesson. Previous heroines learnt the importance of silence, and considerateness through their actions; Fanny learns it through her own stillness. It is at Portsmouth, where the important virtues are most lacking, that Jane Austen most clearly expresses her understanding of the nature of those values which determine good behaviour and manners.

> She could think of nothing but Mansfield, its beloved inmates, its happy ways. Everything where she was now was in full contrast to it. The elegance, propriety, regularity, harmony – and perhaps, above all, the peace and tranquillity of Mansfield were brought to her remembrance every hour of the day, by the prevalence of everything opposite to that here.
>
> (Vol. III, Ch. 8)

The small, angry, loud, unnecessary movements of the house in Portsmouth are written large in the huge changes in society that Austen sees and despairs of. The chaos of Portsmouth is not just about money, for the family are lower middle class and have servants. They are far from poor. The despair in the house is moral, not physical, in its nature. Both parents have abandoned their duties, just as in society at large the economic and social changes mean that, as Jane Austen sees it, those who should regulate and control their society have also given up and failed in their duty.

London too, although it never actually enters the pages of the novel, is another emblem of what is wrong in society. Mary and Henry Crawford have spent much of their time in London and have acquired their moral weaknesses from living in the city. The Crawfords come to represent all that Austen regards as wrong with modern society and its values, seeking only amusement, practising deception, understanding only the value of money and rank and recognising none of the claims of good society. Mrs Grant expresses her hope that Mansfield will cure them, as if their life in London is a sickness which the medicine of rural life can cure. The family at Mansfield Park have had no contact with London, since Lady Bertram is too indolent to visit, but one of the small joys for Maria in her marriage is that she is now able to have a place in London – and it is in London that she gives in to the morally disastrous temptations that destroy her. Julia, too, finds the licence to behave badly and elopes with Yates, and Tom is almost brought to his death by his life in the city. It is significant that Mansfield starts its process of breakdown at the moment when the two city dwellers come to the area and impose their ways on the family.

But what is so unstable about Mansfield Park that one pair of Londoners can disrupt it so quickly and almost bring it to the ground? At its head stands Sir Thomas Bertram, a man who stands aloof from his children and feels pride in their accomplishments and attractiveness but who fails to go beyond their surface gloss. They behave well, are proud of themselves and their place, have excellent manners but lack any sense of humility or self-understanding. In addition, his own values are slightly suspect. We know his wealth is based on the slave trade and that Mansfield is a new house. He is, perhaps, only recently a member of the landed classes and has bought his way in with the gains from his venture capitalism. This does not constitute a criticism of him but what does, in Austen's moral universe, is that he allows Maria to marry a fool, knowing that she could not love him, out of respect for his claims to an ancient aristocracy. He sees a connection with old money as an advantage which presumably outweighs the miseries that will come from his daughter being involved with such a thoughtless man. With the exception of Edmund, Thomas Bertram's children are subdued in his presence and behave well out of cowardice rather than duty. As soon as he goes away their lack of any moral code exposes itself. The worst criticism to lay at his feet, and the most important, is that he allowed the thoroughly nasty Mrs Norris to take charge of his household. It is she who has taught his daughters to be proud, who interferes in almost every aspect of the running of the house, who makes Fanny's life burdensome, and who encourages Maria's marriage. When he discovers that Fanny has refused Henry Crawford he can see only the social and financial benefits of such a marriage. He has no understanding of her feelings and no ability to see what is wrong with Crawford.

His wife is probably the most morally disreputable of the three sisters. She has abandoned her entire life to others, cannot make a decision for herself and is utterly immobile throughout the novel. It is she, who should be in charge of her children, who is content to have Mrs Norris take charge. When even she realises the worth of her niece it is in her own terms. She greets the returning Fanny at the door, actually getting up to do so:

> By one of the suffering party within they were expected with such impatience as she had never known before. Fanny had scarcely passed the solemn-looking servants, when Lady Bertram came from the drawing-room to meet her; came with

no indolent step; and falling on her neck, said, "Dear Fanny! now I shall be comfortable."

(Vol. III, Ch. 16)

She has exchanged her comfortable sofa for a comfortable niece: Fanny is no more to her than her dog or her cushions.

If Sir Thomas is able to impose stillness on his household without being able to inculcate any understanding of the value of that stillness, Lady Bertram is stillness taken to its utter extreme – indolence.

Mrs Norris is one of the great villains of literature on account of being utterly believable. She has insinuated herself into the great house of her sister, exploited Lady Bertram's torpor and deceived Sir Thomas into thinking that her meddlesome behaviour and self-aggrandising greediness are beneficial to him. She meddles for no better reason than that she can. She has no understanding of the consequences of what she does and seeks only to buttress her own sense of self-importance. She is a classic bully, picking on the weakest and most vulnerable. Far worse than her encouragement of Maria in her engagement, and her flattery of her Bertram nieces, is her treatment of Fanny. She brings her to Mansfield Park and treats her badly because she can. She has no thought for Fanny's future or present well-being and actively discourages any kindness towards her. Her malevolence towards Fanny is as inexplicable as her determining that Fanny should never have a fire lit in the old schoolroom. Her punishment at the novel's conclusion is to be sent away with Maria where she has no further meddling to do.

Mrs Norris is in her element in the trip to Sotherton, an event which at times achieves a symbolic representation of all that is wrong with Mansfield Park, and society in general. We have seen how in *Northanger Abbey* 'improvements' become synonymous with the gradual wearing down of the structures which held Austen's idea of society together. General Tilney's improvements are selfish and aimed at profit rather than the good of society. Here we see more of the then current vogue for improvements. The fashion of the time was for the intricate formal gardens of the eighteenth century to give way to artificially created wildernesses, manufactured ruins and sweeping vistas. It is not that Jane Austen disapproves of such vistas, for Pemberly has lots of them. It is the artificiality and interference and the tampering, that she dislikes, just as she portrays Mrs Norris, and the Crawfords' interferences and tampering in the lives of the Mansfield family as malign. Here where Mr Rushworth, ignorant of what he possesses, wishes to alter and improve, we see the Crawfords at the same work on Julia, Maria and Edmund. The day trip has already created passions that only Fanny is aware of, with the two sisters fighting for Crawford's attention, and Mrs Norris' attempts to prevent Fanny from going.

Once there the whole group finds the place oppressive. Mary discovers that Edmund is to be a clergyman, which puts him beyond her vision of a suitable husband, and in twos and threes the young people stray out into the gardens. At the point where the formal gardens end they meet a locked gate and Fanny, exhausted physically and morally by the strains of the day, watching what she knows nobody else can see, sinks to a bench. She is abandoned by Edmund and Mary who go off along a "serpentine" walk, where Mary figures in the allegory of the day as the tempter, seducing Edmund away from his vocation. Rushworth, Maria and Crawford appear, and Rushworth returns to find a key for the gate. Crawford too becomes the tempter offering to help Maria break away from the confines of the formal walk by escaping into the wilderness beyond. She takes his offer, ignoring Fanny's warning: "You will hurt yourself Miss Bertram ... you will certainly hurt yourself against those spikes. You will tear your gown – you will be in danger of slipping into the ha ha. You had better not go." This, of course, is a foreshadowing of exactly what does happen to Maria when she goes off with Crawford. A few minutes later Julia arrives and takes off into the wilderness too, leaving Fanny, passive, alone, and sure in her sense of propriety. Being right all the time can be a very lonely business. The day ends with most people, except Mrs Norris, dissatisfied and no improvements decided at all.

As a teenager, while she lived at Steventon, Jane Austen and her family often took part in amateur theatricals in their home, painting scenery and writing their own plays. Many scenes from her novels could (and regularly are) played out in front of cameras with little or no change to their basic dramatic structure. She clearly liked the theatre. What then do we make of Fanny's horror at the theatricals which take place at Mansfield Park? These theatricals take on a significance which goes far beyond some young people dressing up in the privacy of their own home. Sir Thomas is absent and there is a general air among the children that restraints have been lifted. The Crawfords have brought a sense of daring to the girls, and the two of them, one engaged to be married, are set against each other by Henry Crawford. Here in the play is an opportunity for them to act out their suppressed feelings and desires and it is significant that the play they choose is *Lovers' Vows*, a scandalous one, dealing with seduction and abandonment, illegitimacy, and almost lewd behaviour. In many ways the play's plot reflects what is happening in Sir Thomas' absence: a daughter is betrothed to a wealthy idiot; a clergyman and a beautiful heiress court one another; and, foreshadowing what will happen, a woman is seduced and abandoned. The play offers both Henry and Mary the opportunity for expressing their desires, Henry for flirting outrageously with Maria and creating jealousies between the sisters and Mary for leading on Edmund, making him so attracted to her that he abandons all sense of the proprieties and takes part in the play, in order, he says, to prevent Mary having to act some passionate scenes with another man. Finally, even Fanny is drawn into the Crawfords' schemes as the whole family is set into agitation, with Julia sulking and Mrs Norris organising. The library, the very heart of the authority in the house, is turned about and everyone nags Fanny to take part. Worst of all, Fanny has to watch as Edmund and Mary rehearse their lines, knowing that with every word she is losing Edmund to the skills of her rival for his love. All the family are caught up in the activity and only Fanny stands apart, seeing the distress and upheaval it is causing, being appealed to by first one, then the other, for assistance and knowing the long-term harm it is causing.

The talk ranges around inviting other outsiders to the house and already Mr Yates, an idle but wealthy young man, a member of the aristocracy, has been brought to the house. Mr Yates represents what for Austen was wrong with English society, for here is the aristocracy wasting its energy on dissipation and abandoning its proper role as stewards of the countryside. At the peak of the passion, when even Fanny is being compromised, Sir Thomas unexpectedly returns to meet Mr Yates in costume in his library, ranting his lines. Mr Yates is immediately the 'easy' son of a lord once again and politely gets out of the way. The library is put back, Mr Yates leaves and the play is abandoned, not because anyone has recognised the harm it was causing but because the figure of authority has returned. Even Tom later describes the need for the theatricals as a disease: "brought ... from Ecclesford, and it spread as these things always spread, you know."

For Mary and Henry, the theatricals represent their finest hour when all was movement and activity and pretence, and afterwards even Edmund feels the loss of its liveliness. The corruption of the Crawfords has come very close to damaging the family at Mansfield Park and it is not yet over. Henry's need for activity ruins his chances with Fanny and destroys Maria's reputation and marriage, Mary exposes her inner emptiness to Edmund, makes him unhappy and disappears from the story forever. The core of the family, with Fanny now recognised for all her worth, survives the encroachments of modern life.

5

Emma

Jane Austen was quoted by her nephew, James Edward Austen-Leigh, many years after the publication of *Emma*, as saying, "I am going to take a heroine whom no-one but myself will much like". *Emma* is a story about a doted-on, wealthy, beautiful young woman whose future is assured, and whose only object in life seems to be meddling in other people's lives. She temporarily ruins the happiness of a worthy, hard-working, young man and, as part of this process, manages to make a simple, unaffected young woman proud and unsatisfied. As if this is not enough, Emma is rude to a poor old woman, gossips about a penniless girl whose skills and beauty are greater than her own, and competes in snobbery with an upstart from Bristol. To add to the charge sheet, she succeeds, if only unintentionally, in leading on a clergyman, flirts publicly with a man she has no feelings for, and quarrels with the man she should have realised loved her. Despite all this, she finally comes to be rewarded for her snobbery, bitchiness, gossiping and flirting, by winning the hand and heart of the finest, richest man in Highbury.

Nothing much happens in *Emma*. There is a Christmas party at Randalls, just half a mile or so from Emma's house and a dinner party at the Coles'. Emma has her own dinner party, there is a ball at the Crown Inn, a strawberry picking day at Donwell Abbey and a trip to Box Hill. The only other 'event' to be noted is the fact that Harriet is scared by some travellers.

For a novel so short on action, there are far more characters than usually appear in a novel by Austen. Besides the main players, the whole of Highbury society appears in this novel. We have Robert Martin and his sisters, a tenant farming family on Mr Knightley's estate, and Doctor Perry and his family. There are the Coles, in trade and wealthy but socially below Emma's radar, and William Larkins, Mr Knightley's estate manager. As well as Mrs Goddard and her whole school full of girls and teachers, there is Mrs Stokes at the Crown Inn and the poor but worthy family that Emma visits. There is also the traveller community, as well as the family at Maple Grove and their neighbours, the Sucklings, Frank's adopted family, the Campbells, and Isabella's family and doctor in London. Emma herself is as trapped in this society as much as she is a part of it. When she makes enemies of the Eltons she will have to live with it forever, and if her meddling in Harriet's life causes harm to herself that also will always be with her.

Unlike *Pride and Prejudice*, where we are frequently regaled with the opinions of Meryton society and where the author moves seamlessly from the inner thoughts of one character to another, here we are only given Emma's point of view and it is a foolish reader who is as surprised as Emma to find her accosted by Mr Elton in her father's carriage.

So why would Jane Austen want to write about a group of mediocre villagers, a spoiled snob, her irritating father, and the rest of them? Not because she has an exciting tale to tell, or grand passions to display. Yet this is Austen at her peak. She has moved on from the bright, sparkling, easy-to-love Elizabeth Bennet, and in *Mansfield Park* has written a novel that dares to pronounce on the state of England. She has not yet quite moved into the cynicism of *Persuasion* and *Sanditon*. The mature, acclaimed novelist is looking back at 21 instead of laughing at us through it. *Emma* is a kind of romantic mystery story too, a who loves who rather than a whodunit. As with any good detective story, the signs are all there for an alert reader to spot. There is Mr Elton's fawning, where he places the riddle, his strange reactions to Harriet's illness and John Knightley pointing this out to Emma herself. Later we have Frank Churchill's constant suggestions that his mother-in-law should visit the Bates, the interruptions of seemingly innocent scenes between himself and Jane Fairfax, his almost telling Emma about the engagement and Emma's admiration of Mr Knightley at the ball.

Another reading of this novel, at odds with the detective story genre, highlights its fineness as lying in the fact that from the very beginning, the discerning reader knows what the outcome of this story will be. When Emma announces that she will never marry we know that the story will be about her courtship and marriage; when she sits down on the first evening to tea with a man who is her equal in rank and an old comfortable friend we know who she will marry. From this perspective, the pleasure in reading the story is the process by which Emma comes to understand what the author has been signalling to us from the very beginning. As Emma's story progresses we hear Mr Knightley's reproaches for her behaviour and it is his rebuke which eventually brings her to her moral senses, and we, suspecting otherwise, laugh while she imagines that she has lost the man she loves.

Like Austen's other heroines, Emma learns the art of living a thoughtful, considerate life but unlike the others all the setbacks to this process are of her own making. Elizabeth is harmed by a badly behaved family and the behaviour of others. Once she knows the truth about things she can judge correctly. Eleanor and Marianne and Catherine, like Fanny and Anne, are affected by their circumstances to important degrees but, unlike them, all the things that create Emma's problems are of her own making.

Emma has a very sizeable, personal fortune of £30,000. She lives in a very small community, made up of good-natured but mild-mannered, boring, malleable neighbours and friends – Harriet, Mrs and Mr Weston, Mr Woodhouse – none of whom are likely to provide any opposition to Emma and her plans. The two people who do stand out with any strength of character are the two Knightley brothers, both of whom tell Emma at various times that she is unaware of the consequences of her actions. Emma has an obligation to humour a very annoying man, her father, which she does gracefully and compassionately. She says of herself:

> "There is no charm equal to tenderness of heart," … "There is nothing to be compared to it. Warmth and tenderness of heart, with an affectionate, open manner, will beat all the clearness of head in the world, for attraction, I am sure it will. It is tenderness of heart which makes my dear father so generally beloved – which gives Isabella all her popularity. – I have it not – but I know how to prize and respect it. – Harriet is my superior in all the charm and all the felicity it gives."
>
> (Vol. II, Ch. 13)

Emma knows one of her faults at least. Her problem is that caring for her father is her only occupation. She lives in a stultifyingly boring village where few newcomers enliven the days and very little ever happens. Unlike less well-endowed young women she has no potential husbands to attract and consequently there is little incentive to maintain an interest in being good at the piano. She has also abandoned drawing, and even reading, and badly needs a distraction. In order to engage her active mind and fulfil what might be charitably called an artistic need to create, she turns to storytelling. Emma makes up stories from the people around her. She even admits it to herself when delighting in the story of Harriet's rescue by Frank Churchill:

> Such an adventure as this,—a fine young man and a lovely young woman thrown together in such a way, could hardly fail of suggesting certain ideas to the coldest heart and the steadiest brain. So Emma thought, at least. Could a linguist, could a grammarian, could even a mathematician have seen what she did, have witnessed their appearance together, and heard their history of it, without feeling that circumstances had been at work to make them peculiarly interesting to each other? – How much more must an imaginist, like herself, be on fire with speculation and foresight! – especially with such a groundwork of anticipation as her mind had already made.
> (Vol. III, Ch. 3)

She invents Mr Elton's attraction to Harriet, Jane Fairfax's affair, Frank Churchill's attraction to herself and Harriet's love of Frank Churchill. Most of all she makes up a story about herself, namely that she will never marry. Harriet is particularly useful to Emma the storyteller because she is a blank page on which Emma can write almost any story she likes. Harriet's mysterious origins allow Emma to invent a romantic, high-born liaison for her and her lack of personality and depth allows Emma to feel that a choice of husband for her is not too circumscribed by the need for compatibility or the suitability of a particular character type. Harriet, lacking the confidence to say otherwise, goes along with all of Emma's stories for her, until she decides that Mr Knightley loves her and then all Emma's stories come crashing down around her. Most of all, Harriet offers Emma risk-free entertainment. Like Elizabeth Bennet, Emma shies away from commitment and the risk of giving in to her own tenderness of heart can be displaced by a substitute in the form of the affectionate and loving Harriet.

The person with whom Emma might naturally form a more balanced relationship is Jane Fairfax, her intellectual equal, but Jane stands as a permanent reproach to Emma. She is cultured, talented, beautiful and has applied herself in a way that Emma abandoned years before. She is what Emma ought to be, a constant reminder to Emma's conscience both by her beauty and talent and her need for Emma's attention and friendship.

Emma is a snob but her snobbery is not that of people who are insecure in their position in society and who cling to their assumed status by putting down those they believe are below them socially. Emma has no such insecurity and her snobbery is not of this vulgar kind. Everyone recognises her as the most important figure in their society. When she says of Robert Martin:

> The yeomanry are precisely the order of people with whom I feel I can have nothing to do. A degree or two lower, and a creditable appearance might interest me; I might hope to be useful to their families in some way or other. But a farmer can need none of my help, and is, therefore, in one sense, as much above my notice as in every other he is below it.
>
> (Vol. I, Ch. 4)

She is speaking with utter confidence and an element of truth. Robert Martin has no need for social contact with her and there is nothing she can do for him. Her reason for disliking Robert Martin is not that he is below her in rank but that he will take Harriet, her latest plaything, away.

Emma looks down on the Coles, who in wealth are almost her equal, because they are nouveau riche and because they are attempting to move up in Highbury society:

> The Coles were very respectable in their way, but they ought to be taught that it was not for them to arrange the terms on which the superior families would visit them. This lesson, she very much feared, they would receive only from herself; she had little hope of Mr Knightley, none of Mr Weston.
>
> (Vol. II, Ch. 7)

In the event, Emma is hurt by the lack of an invitation to their dinner party and far from being able to put the upstarts in their place, attends the dinner gratefully when she is finally invited. Perhaps Emma sees the possibility that her control and influence are waning and her snobbery stems from that fear. Neither Mr Knightley nor Mr Weston share her views of the importance of rank since both accept the Coles' invitations regularly and Mr Knightley has great admiration for Robert Martin. Emma looks down on Mrs and Miss Bates too:

> She had had many a hint from Mr Knightley and some from her own heart, as to her deficiency – but none were equal to counteract the persuasion of its being very disagreeable, – a waste of time – tiresome women – and all the horror of being in danger of falling in with the second-rate and third-rate of Highbury, who were calling on them for ever, and therefore she seldom went near them.
>
> (Vol. II, Ch. 1)

She thinks a marriage between Jane Fairfax and Mr Knightley would be degrading to him and when she discovers that Harriet was the natural daughter only of a tradesman, and not a person of higher rank, her opinion turns against her too.

> Such was the blood of gentility which Emma had formerly been so ready to vouch for! – It was likely to be as untainted, perhaps, as the blood of many a gentleman: but what a connexion had she been preparing for Mr. Knightley – or for the Churchills – or even for Mr Elton! – The stain of illegitimacy, unbleached by nobility or wealth, would have been a stain indeed.
>
> (Vol. III, Ch. 19)

Emma never entirely loses her snobbery for this sentiment is expressed in the final paragraphs of the novel, expressed by the new, improved heroine. Emma, finally, has to be accepted for who she is. She cannot help the way she attaches an unnecessarily exaggerated importance to an individual's social class. She is not perfect but she does learn not to judge others purely in terms of their place in the social ladder. If Jane Austen's heroines learn from their prospective husbands, what Emma learns from Mr Knightley is to stop talking, to stop making up stories, to stop meddling and to value worth rather than be blinded by class. She tells her father, who has misunderstood a conversation with Mr Knightley, that it is all just fun: "it is all a joke – we always say what we like to one another". Mr Knightley does not joke or invent things in this way. He sees the danger of her storytelling and tries repeatedly to warn her about it.

How then is Emma different from Mary and Henry Crawford, another pair of attractive, wealthy meddlers? Emma is kind to the poor while Mary Crawford takes pity on Fanny when all are nagging her to join the theatricals. Emma likes games but so does Mary. Both like dinner parties and teasing conversation and both arrange the marriages of others, or try to. Emma tries to arrange Harriet's matrimonial prospects and Mary works on her brother and Fanny. Mary makes crass remarks about her uncle; Emma about Miss Bates. Why, as the novel draws to its conclusions, is Emma not punished by the author, as Mary Crawford is, by being sent away from the good people?

The difference between Emma and the Crawfords is, of course, that Emma learns from her mistakes. She possesses a moral core that is lacking in Mary, even if, like Elizabeth Bennet, she learns in fits and starts and spends much of her time refusing to believe what she has learned. She begins her fantasy story about Harriet soon after meeting her and when her plans are brought to an abrupt halt, by the near engagement of Harriet to Robert Martin, she decides that the man is an oaf:

> He is plain, undoubtedly – remarkably plain – but that is nothing compared with his entire want of gentility. I had no right to expect much, and I did not expect much; but I had no idea that he could be so very clownish, so totally without air.
> (Vol. I, Ch. 4)

This contrasts with her earlier assessment of him that she made to herself: "His appearance was very neat, and he looked like a sensible young man." Later, when she reads his letter of proposal to Harriet, she again refuses to accept what she knows in her heart to be true:

> The style of the letter was much above her expectation. There were not merely no grammatical errors, but as a composition

it would not have disgraced a gentleman; the language though plain, was strong and unaffected, and the sentiments it expressed very much to the credit of the writer. It was short but expressed good sense, warm attachment, liberality, propriety, even delicacy of feeling.

(Vol. I, Ch. 7)

Emma is brought to silence by her own realisation that this is the letter of a gentleman, if not in rank then certainly in feeling. She is quick to rationalize what is not acceptable and a few seconds allows her to make up another story; his sisters helped him write it. Even then she has to argue with herself about it, admitting it not to be in a female style, that the writer is "vigorous, decided, with sentiments to a certain point, not coarse".

Emma's making up of stories is too important to her for an admission that she is meddling, even though Mr Knightley tells her angrily the harm she has done. She carries on with her plans through the business of framing Harriet's portrait, the riddle passed to her by Mr Elton, the subterfuge with the broken shoelace aimed at bringing the two together until the first volume ends in the crisis of Mr Elton's proposal. Emma is set back by the event but not deterred. As she sits alone in her room, her first thought is outraged pride that an upstart like Mr Elton should aspire to propose marriage to her. Long after her hurt pride subsides a little, she begins to think of the harm she has done to Harriet and blames herself:

> The first error and the worst lay at her door. It was foolish, it was wrong, to take so active a part in bringing any two people together. It was adventuring too far, assuming too much, making light of what ought to be serious, a trick of what ought to be simple. She was quite concerned and ashamed, and resolved to do such things no more.

(Vol. I, Ch. 16)

In the very next paragraph she begins to plan Harriet's next adventure. This first crisis brought about by Emma's meddling has done nothing to stop her interference in other people's lives and her next target for Harriet's affection, after she has decided that he will not do for Miss Woodhouse, is Frank Churchill. Her conscience still tells her that she is behaving badly and she witnesses for herself the harm that her interference is causing when she lets Harriet off for 15 minutes to visit her old friends:

> Emma could not but picture it all, and feel how justly they might resent, how naturally Harriet must suffer. It was a bad business. She would have given a great deal, or endured a great deal, to have had the Martins in a higher rank of life.
> (Vol. II, Ch. 5)

Emma knows here that she has behaved badly and, greatly dissatisfied with herself, goes off to visit Randalls where no one ever finds fault with her.

In almost every other instance of Emma's meddling she is aware of it, but puts the feelings aside because she is having so much fun. She feels shame after gossiping about Jane Fairfax:

> She doubted whether she had not transgressed the duty of woman by woman in betraying her suspicions of Jane Fairfax's feelings to Frank Churchill. It was hardly right; but it had been so strong an idea, that it would escape her, and his (Frank Churchill's) submission to all that she told, was a compliment to her penetration which made it difficult for her to be quite certain that she ought to have held her tongue.
> (Vol. II, Ch. 9)

While Mary Crawford has no such qualms about her behaviour, Emma has a moral core and knows every time she meddles in other people's lives. She chooses to suppress her feelings until, after her apotheosis of meddling at Box Hill, where she blurts out a joke at Miss Bates' expense, she is mortified and the process of change in Emma's behaviour slowly begins.

In the meantime, though, her meddling progresses apace when she decides she does not love Frank Churchill but that he will do for Harriet and her encouragement of Harriet in that direction, misunderstood by Harriet as encouragement to consider Mr Knightley as her suitor leads to the possibility that Harriet might get an offer from Mr Knightley. But before this horror comes the day out at Box Hill when Emma and her friends spend the day wandering. All the signs are there – the company has left its familiar surroundings and with them it leaves behind the practices and conventions that help hold their society together – that Austen flags up when she is dealing with a fracturing of the delicate social equilibrium. Matters become nasty, with the company breaking up into two groups. Emma is dissatisfied with the day, it is stiflingly hot and Frank is loud and boorish, and she commits the great sin of blurting out, in the form of a joke, how she feels about Miss Bates and her constant chatter. The moment passes and Emma moves on to other things, apparently unmoved by her indiscretion. It is only when Mr Knightley criticises her that she realises what she has done:

> You, whom she had known from an infant, whom she had seen grow up from a period when her notice was an honour, to have you now, in thoughtless spirits, and the pride of the moment, laugh at her, humble her—and before her niece, too—and before others, many of whom (certainly *some*,) would be entirely guided by *your* treatment of her.
>
> (Vol. III, Ch. 7)

Emma is a reformed character, although clearly more affected by Mr Knightley's bad opinion of her than by the injury she has done to Miss Bates. She is moved for the first time by Jane Fairfax's position, unaware as yet that it is she herself who has caused much of Jane's suffering, but her efforts to help are turned away. Emma finds herself living with the consequences of her meddling which culminates in Harriet's announcement that Mr Knightley is about to propose marriage. Emma's transformation is complete. She now knows where her true destiny lies and the story quickly resolves itself. She, hardly changed at all, still an imaginist and a bit of a snob, marries the man she deserves. Harriet, fortunately, is unharmed by her meddling and Jane Fairfax is happily married, although you have to wonder what kind of a husband Frank Churchill will turn out to be when he spent so much time publicly flirting with another woman.

The one area where the reformed Emma can approve of herself and give herself some credit for showing some affection is towards her father. Mr Woodhouse, needy, over-solicitous, febrile and convinced that his views on everything from gruel to marriage are the only true ones, may be one of the novel's caricatures but it is not clear how he should be read. Is he an amusing, kindly old man filled with generous but unnecessary concern for others, or he is a drain on

Emma, a meddler who tries to force his ideas on others and a man who dislikes marriage. The critic Marvin Mudrick in *Irony as Form* (1952) sees him as a "parasitic plant ... a ... barely living excuse for Emma's refusal to commit herself to the human world." Does Emma's decision to remain at Hartfield show that she has not fundamentally changed or does it show her generosity of spirit? This point of view seems too severe and unforgiving for Mr Woodhouse's concerns are all about trivial things, like not getting your feet wet, eating bland food, the risks involved in driving in bad weather and, though he almost causes an argument with his son-in-law over the benefits of a seaside holiday and has perfectly good food sent away when entertaining Mrs Bates, he is harmless, an extreme form of what many elderly people become. If he is a parasite, he is one whom many of his neighbours respect. Such respect is mutual and Mr Woodhouse is keenly aware of the need to subordinate his personal opinions to the higher interests of his social obligations. He articulates this in his response to Emma's teasing of him for hating marriage but paying such respect to brides:

> "No, my dear, I never encouraged any body to marry, but I would always wish to pay every proper attention to a lady – and a bride, especially, is never to be neglected. More is avowedly due to *her*. A bride, you know, my dear, is always the first in company, let the others be who they may ... This is a matter of mere common politeness and good-breeding, and has nothing to do with any encouragement to people to marry."
> (Vol. II, Ch. 14)

Mr Woodhouse understands this respect for other people in a way that his daughter, until her change of heart after Box Hill, does not.

An interesting figure in this novel is Jane Fairfax. She stands as a permanent reproach to Emma because of her silence, her accomplishments and because Emma could bring some pleasantness into her life but declines to do so. While Emma's future is an open one (she may actually choose not to marry and she has friends and a place in society), Jane Fairfax's is not. Deprived of the social advantages given to Emma, and like Fanny Price in *Mansfield Park* or Mrs Smith in *Persuasion*, she quietly accepts what might happen to her. Her only hope for a future without the drudgery of being bought and sold as a governess lies in her secret engagement to Frank Churchill. In many ways she is a shadowy figure, represented only through Emma's eyes, silent for the most part, and we come to appreciate her position mainly through Emma's own recognition of her plight:

> The contrast between Mrs Churchill's importance in the world, and Jane Fairfax's, struck her; one was every thing, the other nothing—and she sat musing on the difference of woman's destiny ...
>
> (Vol. III, Ch. 8)

While Jane Fairfax's plight echoes to some extent the position of some women in other Austen novels, Mr Knightley's position is not comparable to any of the men in the other books. His maleness is altogether different to Darcy's. In *Pride and Prejudice*, the master of Pemberly remains shadowy, his motives and feelings held in so much that we have to rely on his housekeeper and his activities offstage to believe he is a good man. Part of the mystery of that novel's love story is that lively Elizabeth should have gained the affection of this deep, reserved man. Mr Knightley, by comparison, is active, forthright, terse, commanding, considerate and has a temper which he keeps wonderfully in check. Only occasionally – "he is a person I never think of from one month's end to another" – does he give vent to his suppressed jealousy and contempt for Frank Churchill. He is the perfect foil to Emma's wilfulness and in one of the final conversations between them we hear the strength of both their characters:

> "Do you dare say this?" cried Mr Knightley. "Do you dare to suppose me so great a blockhead, as not to know what a man is talking of? What do you deserve?"
> "Oh! I always deserve the best treatment, because I never put up with any other;"
>
> (Vol. III, Ch. 18)

A comparison of the love affairs of Elizabeth Bennet and Emma Woodhouse makes clear the degree to which Austen has improved her art. Both heroines come to love a man they have known through the course of the respective stories but for Elizabeth it is a man she meets rarely and even more rarely has any private conversations with, whereas with Emma it is a man she has known all her life, regularly has private conversations with and whose company she looks forward to and enjoys. The plot of *Pride and Prejudice*, and occasionally the tone, is contrived in order to bring the two together, to provide a reason for Elizabeth to reappraise her feelings. Emma's feelings do not change and the irony and humour in the story is that Emma loves Mr Knightley from the very beginning of the story but she does not acknowledge this for what it is. Elizabeth Bennet has a great deal of thinking and considering to do before she arrives at a satisfactory conclusion, whereas Emma's conclusion stares her and the reader in the face from the first chapter. In *Pride and Prejudice* Elizabeth learns something about the nature of judging by first impressions; Emma learns a more important lesson, the value of analysing one own motives.

Mr Knightley differs from Austen's other male figures in that occasionally we are party to his inner thoughts. He suspects an understanding between Jane and Frank and during a walk notices a slip on Frank's part. Frank introduces a topic – the Coles' new carriage – which he could not have known about except through his understanding with Jane. The incident passes beyond all the other figures but Mr Knightley observes both Frank and Jane. Before we become truly a party to his thoughts Austen, like a true detective story writer, having marked the clue which she will return to later, slips easily away into omniscient narrator mode.

Although Emma says that she and Mr Knightley joke together, his remarks to Emma are always serious criticisms and the pair seem as likely to make a go of their marriage as are Elizabeth and Darcy. Emma enjoys imagining, Knightley is a straight talker; she makes a joke of everything, he treats things seriously; she, even at the end of the novel, is still capable of lacking care for others while he shows consideration in everything he does.

Mrs Elton, caricature that she is, is Emma's counterpart. They share, in different degrees and inflections, a predilection for snobbery, a lack of tenderness, a need to pull rank and a belief that they are the very centre of all that is important in Highbury. Mrs Elton is what Emma might be without her beauty, intelligence or wealth. Perhaps that is why she makes Emma so angry:

"A little upstart, vulgar being, with her Mr E., and her *caro sposo*, and her resources, and all her airs of pert pretension and underbred finery. Actually to discover that Mr Knightley is a gentleman! I doubt whether he will return the compliment, and discover her to be a lady. I could not have believed it! And to propose that she and I should unite to form a musical club! One would fancy we were bosom friends!"

(Vol. II, Ch. 14)

Mrs Elton, as befits a caricature, is a one-note figure. Her talk is all about her clothes and her rank and her rich relatives. Her interference in Jane Fairfax's life is not cruelty: it causes hurt to Jane but as a side effect, and her only wish is to show her own power and influence. She lacks sensitivity of the heart and any genuine consideration for the feelings of others but the injury she causes has an innocence that forbids too sharp a criticism of her nature. She becomes ever more of a caricature by the time of the strawberry picking, when her words are dovetailed into a stream of babble, with no-one listening and no reply needed:

" ... abundance about Bristol – Maple Grove – cultivation – beds when to be renewed – gardeners thinking exactly different – no general rule – gardeners never to be put out of their way – delicious fruit – only too rich to be eaten much of – inferior to cherries – currants more refreshing – only objection to gathering strawberries the stooping – glaring sun – tired to death – could bear it no longer – must go and sit in the shade."

(Vol. II, Ch. 6)

By the end of the novel she is quietly dismissed as unworthy of our attention, reduced to only a few unheard remarks about the lack of finery at Emma's wedding, and not even invited to the marriage ceremony.

Miss Bates, is in some ways, a more interesting character even though she is clearly drawn as a caricature to whom we, with Emma, feel vastly superior and a little irritated by. Unlike the Eltons and many other simply-drawn figures, she is harmless and pours goodwill upon the world at large, seeing the best in everything and at first sight apparently blind to most of what goes on around her. She very rarely actually engages any of the other characters in conversation and, rather like the passage of Mrs Elton's above, she engages in an unanswerable monologue, although not as disconnected as it might seem at first. Each sentence, begun but rarely finished, leads on to the next, in some mysterious way known only to herself: "Upon my word Miss Woodhouse, you look ... how do you like Jane's hair ..." Yet Miss Bates, who is the instrument of Emma's awakening to her own faults, on several occasions shows insights and a self-awareness that Emma might find useful:

> "... I know I do sometimes pop out a thing before I am aware. I am a talker you know; I am rather a talker; and now and then I have let a thing escape me which I should not. I am not like Jane; I wish I were. I will answer for it that she never betrayed the least thing in the world."
>
> (Vol. III, Ch, 5)

Miss Bates' most important role in the novel is to trick both Emma and ourselves into thinking her a mere caricature who will never notice any subtle or unkind remarks about her and who we are all justified in being impatient with. The moment which brings Emma to her senses at Box Hill switches Miss Bates from a one-dimensional babbler to a more fully realised person, a vulnerable human being just like the rest of us. Emma's cutting remark at Box Hill hits home and Miss Bates speaks humbly and with a sudden bout of sense to Mr Knightley:

> "Ah! – well – to be sure. Yes, I see what she means, (turning to Mr Knightley,) and I will try to hold my tongue. I must make myself very disagreeable, or she would not have said such a thing to an old friend."
>
> (Vol. III, Ch. 7)

After Mr Knightley's reproach, Emma is able herself to see Miss Bates as a person and to show some tenderness of heart, although she seems to spend longer thinking about Mr Knightley's bad opinion of her than she does Miss Bates' injury. The next day we again see Miss Bates as a more rounded character when, "civil and humble as usual", though clearly distressed, she chooses not to lie to Emma but tells her truthfully that Jane "... is not able – she is gone into her own room – I want her to lie down upon the bed ... but however she is not; she is walking about the room." There is a simple honesty in her talk which puts Emma, and the reader who has shared her view of Miss Bates, to shame. Our final glimpse of Miss Bates occurs when Emma goes to congratulate Jane on her engagement and her outpourings of bonhomie are even more incoherent:

> "Yes, indeed, I quite understand – dearest Jane's prospects – that is, I do not mean. – But she is charmingly recovered. – How is Mr Woodhouse? – I am so glad. – Quite out of my power. – Such a happy little circle as you find us here. – Yes, indeed. – Charming young man! – that is – so very friendly; I mean good Mr Perry! – such attention to Jane!"
>
> (Vol. III, Ch. 16)

It is worth noting the very formal structure of this novel. Written in three books, as was the custom of the day, each one charts Emma's moral education from self-absorption to a more considerate and mindful woman, aware of the harm that her meddling can do. The books track her progress into Highbury society, in Book I going no further than to her governess' home, in Book II condescending to visit the Coles and then inviting Highbury society into her own home, and then in Book III venturing further and further away from home, with the visit to Donwell, the ball at the Crown Inn and culminating in the disastrous trip to Box Hill. With each event Emma strays further from the seclusion of her life so far and further into her meddling and careless behaviour.

Each book also contains a romance for Emma, followed by a proposal. In the first book there is Mr Elton's misunderstood courtship, in the second her flirtation with Frank Churchill and her realisation that she is not in love with him and finally, in the third book, her realisation of her love for Mr Knightley and his proposal.

Just as the events in Emma's education take place in formal patterns of three, the quality of her mistakes follows the course of the year in which these events take place. The novel begins in the dark, its mock sombre tone matching the wintry late evening. Emma has little to look forward to over the long October and November evenings except her father's company. Harriet comes as a welcome distraction and Emma's meddling with her takes place over the course of the winter and meets its first climax in the dark, freezing journey home to Hartfield. As the year begins to turn, Emma's social circle widens, she meets Frank Churchill, engages in further foolish activities until, in high summer's unpleasant heat, Emma witnesses the unhappiness of both Jane and Frank and then commits the act of folly which brings her to her senses. When Emma discovers that she may have inadvertently brought Harriet and Mr Knightley together, and realises too the harm she has brought to Jane Fairfax, the weather matches her mood:

> The evening of this day was very long, and melancholy, at Hartfield. The weather added what it could of gloom. A cold stormy rain set in, and nothing of July appeared but in the trees and shrubs, which the wind was despoiling, and the length of the day, which only made such cruel sights the longer visible.
>
> (Vol. II, Ch. 12)

Finally, it is a warm July evening when Emma finally makes an honest commitment:

> Never had the exquisite sight, smell, sensation of nature, tranquil, warm, and brilliant after a storm, been more attractive to her. She longed for the serenity they might gradually introduce; and ... she lost no time in hurrying into the shrubbery. – There, with spirits freshened, and thoughts a little relieved, she had taken a few turns, when she saw Mr Knightley passing through the garden door, and coming towards her.
>
> (Vol. III, Ch. 13)

Mr Knightley and Emma, Harriet and Robert Martin and Jane and Frank all marry in the autumn, the season of harvest and fulfilment.

Like the other novels, this one ends in marriage and the heroine is a wiser and happier woman for it. But Highbury remains, and Emma remains a part of it, to encounter Mrs Elton's snobbery on a daily basis, listen patiently to Miss Bates' letters from Jane, endure all the daily rounds of living in a small, polite, humdrum community where nothing much ever happens, just as Jane Austen did.

6

Persuasion

In *Emma*, the effects on a small community of interference are dealt with through a number of instances. There is Emma's incursion into Harriet's life, Mrs Elton's meddling with Jane, Frank's interference with the feelings of Jane, his parents and Emma. Such a list could be continued. *Persuasion* takes up and highlights this theme by focusing on the consequences for a young woman of interference in the form of persuasion.

Persuasion was Jane Austen's final completed novel, written between 1815 and 1816, from the relative comfort of her new home at Chawton Cottage. It was published posthumously, along with *Northanger Abbey*, in 1818. As with *Sense and Sensibility* and *Pride and Prejudice*, the category of abstract nouns provides Austen with a title, though this time the title does not present a twinned set. It is the single concept that concerns the author. In our own times, the power of persuasion infiltrates huge areas of our lives and our consumer culture is premised on the ability of the advertising industry to persuade us as to what we should buy and, more generally, how we should live. Jane Austen examines the nature of persuasion, in her characteristic way, by focusing on a family situation and certain individuals.

In Dr Johnson's dictionary 'persuasion' is "the act of influencing by expostulation; the act of gaining or attempting the passions" and a persuader as someone who appeals to the emotions rather than the reason lies behind Johnson's definition of a persuader as "an importunate advisor". In Richardson's *Sir Charles Grandison*, Austen's favourite novel, the practice of persuasion is viewed as cruel and damaging. The person who comes under the influence of a persuader is harmed, regardless of the degree to which they are persuaded. If they agree to the arguments of their persuader, they have changed their own inclinations and so regret it. If they deny their persuader, they feel the harm they have done to a good friend. In *Persuasion*, someone like Lady Russell, who has persuaded Anne to give up her engagement, means well in her intentions but the outcome is cruel. There is an inherent risk in the act of persuading someone, even if one's intentions are good. What the novel sets out to examine, among other things, is how one can judge whether persuasion is a good thing; how to determine when it is time to be persuaded and when to stick to your own inclinations.

While the nature of persuasion is discussed at crucial moments in the story, this novel differs from the others in that it opens a window on the intimate workings of several households, little social commonwealths, as Anne calls them. In *Pride and Prejudice* we see briefly the rented establishment at Netherfield and get a glimpse of Pemberly but the only home we see functioning is Elizabeth's. So too, *Northanger Abbey*, *Sense and Sensibility*, *Emma* and *Mansfield Park* show us a few homes only briefly. In *Persuasion*, we have Anne's own home, under two different regimes, her sister Mary's home, the Musgroves', her father's new home in Bath, the home of Captain Harville and his wife, and the lodgings of Mrs Smith. This novel is about families and their internal workings and we see them, in their various forms, through the eyes of the solitary Anne, who adapts herself to each family and its affairs, assisting its smooth running and becoming essential to them all, except for her own.

This novel also distinguishes itself in another fundamental way. *Pride and Prejudice, Mansfield Park* and to a lesser extent the other novels accept the right of a certain class of people to exist in a hierarchical society where everyone has his or her place, in an almost feudal-like system, and where order is maintained by observing a set of rules that ensure social cohesion. In *Pride and Prejudice* the old order receives new strength from the adoption of Elizabeth Bennet and in *Mansfield Park* the owners of the Big House learn the true meaning of their place in society while those who fail to understand are sent away forever. In *Emma*, the heroine learns about the proper nature of social roles and the effects of tampering with them. *Persuasion* is different in that it ends with no resolution in this respect. The Big House and the appropriate role of its owner is left open. Its proprietor, Sir Walter, fails to learn about his obligations as a member of the gentry and his house is rented out to people who, the reader suspects, will make a much better job of looking after it. The story ends with the distinct possibility that the wicked William Elliot and his new mistress, Mrs Clay, might one day own Kellynch Hall. Anne herself walks away from what her class position indicates should be her concern and marries a man with little position in society, a mere professional, and she makes friends from the same group of people.

This novel differs too in that its horizons are far wider than those of Highbury or Meryton. They encompass, through the naval community, foreign parts and the heroine herself travels from her home to Lyme and Bath. Also, unlike all her other novels, *Persuasion* is set in Austen's contemporary England. She began writing in 1815 and the beginning of the story is set in the summer of the year before. When Wentworth and the other sailors come home from sea they have returned from a real 12-year-long war against the French, and Wentworth's fortune has been made by taking French naval vessels and selling off the captured goods. When Anne, who might have married Mr Elliot and stayed at her beloved home, abandons her class and security, she attaches herself to a man who, in a future which is unknown both to the heroine and to the author, may go off again at any moment and never return.

Austen's heroines have, until now, learned important lessons about life. Catherine has learned to read beyond the superficiality of appearance, Marianne has learned to temper passion with reason, Elizabeth to read her own feelings better and Emma to stop meddling and look into her own heart. Even the saintly Fanny learns what it means to feel at home. *Persuasion*, though, begins after the heroine has learned her life lesson for, by succumbing to the persuasion of others, she is aware that a chance of happiness was sacrificed and her world reduced to a shallow place. The Anne who marries Wentworth at the novel's conclusion is essentially the same woman who begins the story. What changes is that the other characters in the novel learn to appreciate her value and authority.

The novel opens with Sir Walter reading his favourite book, Debrett's *Baronetage of England*, which gives an account of himself and gives us an indication of what the story is to be about. His own details are egotistically focused on, while the generations who went before him and their years of dedication to their country and estate are brushed over:

> ... serving the office of High Sheriff, representing the borough in three successive parliaments, exertions of loyalty, and dignity of baronet, in the first year of Charles II, with all the Marys and Elizabeths they had married: forming altogether two handsome duodecimo pages.
>
> (Vol. I, Ch. 1)

From the start, Sir Walter is marked out as a vain, shallow man. His interest in the *Baronetage of England* is because it reflects an image of himself that he likes to contemplate, just like the large mirrors he keeps in his dressing room the better to admire himself and the elder daughter who, " very handsome and very like himself" he keeps by his side to reflect back his sense of rank. The same kind of reasoning makes Mrs Clay someone he favours, although her brand of flattery is much more conscious and scheming than his elder daughter's.

His life is about pleasure, and his estates and his house, rank and money are important to him because they contribute to his self-obsessed pleasure-seeking nature. His thoughts are all about display, the importance of being seen, and his greatest anger at Mr Elliot's rejection of his offers of friendship seem to centre around the loss of being seen with him at the House of Commons. To Sir Walter, the House of Commons, the centre of government, is merely a place for display. We are told that while all those around him are giving way to the damage that time wreaks on their appearance, he, at 54, and his elder daughter at 29 were still handsome. Mrs Clay offers an explanation for this:

> ... it is only the lot of those who are not obliged to follow any (profession) who can live in a regular way, in the country, choosing their own hours, following their own pursuits ... without the torment of trying for more; it is only their lot, I say, to hold the blessings of health and a good appearance to the utmost ...
>
> (Vol. I, Ch. 3)

She is saying that it is only those wealthy enough to be completely useless and unproductive, the aristocracy, who remain good looking well into their middle age.

Sir Walter has been so profligate in his ways since the death of his wife that he can no longer afford to run his house and must rent it out. He sees no problem with that for the house has merely been a means to further his enjoyment of himself and his life. He gives the house up with no regrets and the one part of the estate he wishes to keep the newcomers out of are his pleasure gardens.

Sir Walter's opinions of his acquaintances are based purely on their rank. When Mr Wentworth is described as a gentleman he is confused because to Sir Walter a gentleman is a member of his own class, the landed aristocracy, and the man in question was a mere country parson, a nobody in Sir Walter's estimation. His objections to naval men are twofold for not only do they lose their youthful looks too quickly but they are awarded social positions which puts them equal in rank with members of the aristocracy. Sir Walter, the atrophied remnant of a useless class, can only watch with horror as these upstarts, the people who actually do things, get credit for their achievements. Sir Walter approves of Mr William Elliot for his class, his wealth and his manners. He considers him as another reflection of himself, in name at least, and thus a suitable husband for his favourite daughter. The Musgroves, on the other hand, have no class, belonging as they do to merely a country gentleman's family, with poor manners and no awareness of the rank bestowed upon them by their connection to him. Even Captain Wentworth becomes a nodding acquaintance because now he has rank and wealth and is good looking, all the requirements needed, especially in Bath where who decorates your drawing room is a sign of your social standing.

Sir Walter graces, as he would put it, the first few chapters of the novel and the final ones which take place in Bath. His assessments of his acquaintances are, as seen, based on rank and appearance and those who do not meet his standards are often described as "nobodies". By the novel's end, ironically and fittingly, we realise that it is in fact he who is the nobody. He has no home, no heir, no wife, no son, and no role in life.

From the early chapters set in Kellynch, the plot moves, with its heroine, to Uppercross and the two Musgrove households. From the stultifying and loveless snobbery of Kellynch, we encounter the noisy house of the elder Musgroves with their happy children. The two elder girls are attractive and confident, their lives dedicated to enjoying their home and their extended family. To the Musgroves, entertaining is a pleasure and the poorer relatives are welcome at all times as a source of good company. The girls are both of marriageable age and will choose husbands according to their inclinations and not from a calculation of their possible social standing. One sister marries a poor cousin while the other settles eventually for a lowly ship's captain. The Musgroves have no sense of rank, all are welcome at their home and their lack of respect for rank is a cause for dissension between them and Sir Walter's youngest daughter. As the most recently married member of the family and the wife of the heir, she should be given precedence at formal events such as dinner engagements or balls and the Musgroves seem regularly to forget that. But the Musgroves, another example of the landed gentry that in the Austenian scheme of things have a duty which goes along with their privilege, despite their charms and easy ways, are massively ignorant, uncultured people, who, when they see Charles Hayter surrounded by large books fear that he must be sickening for something. Charles Musgrove is only able to find some good in the quiet, literary Captain Benwick after an afternoon's ratting when he suddenly seems to be a much more worthy person. Nor do they comprehend their own motives. The Musgrove sisters complain to Anne that Mary is always taking precedence, perhaps hoping that Anne could put a word in with Mary. When Mrs Musgrove assures Anne that she can mention any wrongdoings among the servants in her daughter-in-law's house her real interest is in getting some juicy bits of gossip about her daughter-in-law. At Lyme, Henrietta confides to Anne her concern for the health of Dr Shirley whose retirement to the health-giving seaside would make her fiancé better off.

The literal-mindedness of the family shows itself in Louisa who, strongly moved by Frederick Wentworth's eulogy in admiration of a strong will, becomes suddenly headstrong, and it is her refusal to be persuaded at Lyme that brings on her accident.

In the Musgrove household, as in Kellynch, we see an alteration to the perspective that was characteristic of the other novels. In *Sense and Sensibility*, the sisters visit Lady Middleton and find the noise and chaos of a household with children unpleasant. When Anne visits the Musgroves at Christmas, she finds the noise of the family unpleasant but recognises the happy scene they make and the worth of their family life:

> Immediately surrounding Mrs Musgrove were the little Harvilles, whom she was sedulously guarding from the tyranny of the two children from the cottage, expressly arrived to amuse them. On one side was a table, occupied by some chattering girls, cutting up silk and gold paper; and on the other were tressels and trays, bending under the weight of brawn and cold pies, where riotous boys were holding high revel; the whole completed by a roaring Christmas fire, which seemed determined to be heard, in spite of the noise of the others ... It was a fine family piece.
>
> (Vol. II, Ch. 2)

At Uppercross cottage, the fault lines between Musgrove comfort and Elliot formality are laid bare. The husband and wife have little in common, he staying out with his dogs as much as he can and she lying on the sofa feigning illness. The children are badly brought up and the house is poorly run. Like her father, Mary has few parental instincts. She feels the marriages of her two sisters-in-law to "nobodies" to be a slight against the rank which she has brought to the Musgrove family. Mary sees only the superficial. When they discover that the unknown gentleman at the inn was their cousin, she admits that all she remembers of the man is the expensive looking carriage and livery. After Louisa's accident she is worse than useless but insists that she stay to look after Louisa in Anne's place out of sheer jealousy and her sense of the dues that should be accorded to someone of her rank. Her response, when she hears Anne is to marry, is to weigh up its usefulness to herself, calculating that, although she will now have to give precedence to Anne at formal dinners, she has the consolation of knowing that Anne's marriage is better than those of her sisters-in-law. This will reflect well on herself while still being less important than her own eventual status as the householder of Uppercross House, as long as Wentworth isn't honoured with a title.

Other families enter the story. At Lyme we meet the Harvilles, a poor family living in cramped conditions and difficult circumstances, in a tiny lodging house. Their circumstances are much like those of Fanny's parents in *Mansfield Park* but the difference is extraordinary:

> ... rooms so small as none but those who invite from the heart could think capable of accommodating so many ... the sight of all the ingenious contrivances and nice arrangements of Captain Harville, to turn the actual space to the best account, to supply the deficiencies of lodging-house furniture, and defend the windows and doors against the winter storms to be expected ... the common necessaries provided by the owner ... contrasted with some few articles of a rare species of wood, excellently worked up, and with something curious and valuable from all the distant countries Captain Harville had visited ... the picture of repose and domestic happiness ...
> (Vol. I, Ch. 11)

Other homes come into the story – Mrs Smith's lodgings, the Dalrymples' Laura Place, The Crofts in Kellynch Hall, Lady Russell's home. As she encounters each of these homes, Anne adapts herself and becomes as useful to each one as she can, though always an outsider and especially so in her own home.

Anne is a very different heroine to the others in that her story, the equivalent to Elizabeth's or Emma's, happened over seven years ago and ended badly. She barely appears in the novel at all until chapter four, when the story of her romance is told in seven paragraphs. For the large part of Volume I, Anne's speech is reported rather than presented as direct conversation and most of her thoughts are only ever articulated to the reader. As the story progresses, the absent, then silent, Anne gradually becomes more and more central and important not only to us but to the other characters. She grows in confidence as her importance in these families becomes more obvious, both to them and to herself, until the climactic scene where she publicly debates with a man, Captain Harville, on equal terms, about the nature of love and attachment.

Anne is unwanted, and remains so, in her own home. She is "just Anne". She lives every day with the knowledge that she made a mistake by being persuaded out of an engagement, and she reads about the man she turned away becoming more successful and wealthy:

> How eloquent could Anne Elliot have been! how eloquent, at least, were her wishes on the side of early warm attachment, and a cheerful confidence in futurity, against that over-anxious caution which seems to insult exertion and distrust Providence! She had been forced into prudence in her youth, she learned romance as she grew older ...
>
> (Vol. I, Ch. 4)

Anne's life is essentially a silent, sad one. She has no one to whom she can express her feelings. Even as she plays the piano in a happy, love-filled home, she is alone and unloved:

> She knew that when she played she was giving pleasure only to herself; but this was no new sensation. Excepting one short period of her life, she had never, since the age of fourteen, never since the loss of her dear mother, known the happiness of being listened to, or encouraged by any just appreciation or real taste. In music she had been always used to feel alone in the world ...
>
> (Vol. I, Ch. 6)

To the other characters in the novel she is a quiet figure, useful to them as a piano player, companion, listener or babysitter. As she moves from one household to another she adapts, aware that every family has its own sphere of interests and that what is of concern to those at Kellynch is unimportant at the Musgrove residence. But Anne has a secret, inner, passionate life which only we are privy to. In the quotation above, relating her reflections at the piano, all the sadness of her life is given concentrated expression: she is unwanted at home, has lost the mother who would have loved her, she has given up the man who offered her happiness and is surrounded by people who only see her as a resource. She does not, however, give way to self-pity and this sense of sadness is a momentary theme, encompassed within her competence and her adaptability to the different family situations. Anne has made a life for herself after her loss and accommodated herself to it, living through her memories and desires and through small exchanges which have a significance known only to herself and to the reader.

The stability of Anne's shored-up regrets and memories is thrown into turmoil when the Crofts arrive at Kellynch. This is partly because her life as she has known it since her loss at age 19 is now ended and she is to become, like her father, a transient. Equally, if not more, significant, the Crofts will bring Captain Wentworth back into her company. There is no hope in this for her of reconciliation with him; she only expects hurt. Each encounter with him passes, unknown to the other, lively, happy characters, as an emotional challenge for her as she fights her passions to remain calm. Only the reader is aware of the emotional chaos going on behind her downcast, quiet exterior. When, while eating breakfast, she meets him for the first time the reader experiences the meeting entirely from Anne's point of view, hearing most of the exchange as she casts her eyes down, unable to even look at him:

> ... the others appeared; they were in the drawing-room. Her eye half met Captain Wentworth's, a bow, a curtsey passed; she heard his voice; he talked to Mary, said all that was right, said something to the Miss Musgroves, enough to mark an easy footing; the room seemed full, full of persons and voices, but a few minutes ended it. Charles shewed himself at the window, all was ready, their visitor had bowed and was gone...
> (Vol. I, Ch. 7)

For all her inner turmoil, she notices his easy manner with the Musgrove daughters and later one of the Musgroves, lively but callous, informs Anne that Wentworth considers her changed beyond recognition. At first mortified, Anne characteristically finds strength in the information, using it to protect herself against the next time she should meet him, crushing any tiny hope that there might still be some feeling left for her.

Anne is a physical, passionate woman and the moments of near contact between her and Wentworth are imbued with a sense of bodily presence. When she spends an evening at the Musgroves in his company the two do not speak, but even with downcast eyes she is aware of his nearness when he sits beside her on the sofa. Later, there is the scene where Wentworth lifts her nephew off her back, the child's hands taken from round her neck, her head physically bent down by the child. Anne is overcome with sensation to the point where she must, as soon as politeness allows, leave the room to recover. On their walk she must recover, both from his kindness and his physical nearness, when he hands her into the Crofts' carriage. In Bath, her physical attraction to Captain Wentworth draws her, against her own reason, to the shop doorway where he has just passed by, to get a better look at him. In each of these encounters, Anne does not speak and it is as if the emotions of the past are always between her and her ability to express herself.

A change in Anne's social role begins after the incident at Lyme. Until this point she has been a silent, reflective, unnoticed bundle of controlled passion, responding to tiny gestures and words and barely speaking, just listening politely and sympathetically to others. Her conversations, such as they are, are delivered to us in reported speech. In company, she has been a silent observer to the point where, on the walk to Charles Hayter's house, she becomes a hidden witness to a conversation which she knows is partly about herself. We know her competence, she has taken charge when the nephew is injured, but from this point on the other characters begin to learn her true worth. Here at Lyme she becomes beautiful again and comes under the admiring eye of a stranger, bringing this new beauty to the attention of Wentworth. She is able to provide a sympathetic ear to Henrietta while smiling to herself about Henrietta's true motives. She engages in a conversation with another withdrawn person, Captain Benwick, although still through the medium of reported speech, and is able to advise him on the nature of sadness and loss. After the accident, while her sister becomes hysterical and Henrietta faints away, Anne takes charge and is able to deal with the situation while the others are overcome. The reactions of the men who are present are of no more help than the women, what with Charles sobbing and Captain Wentworth staggering against a wall and then attempting to run off to find a surgeon in a town where he is a stranger. Anne and the Harvilles are the only people capable of rational action, taking charge of both the unconscious Louisa and her hysterical friends.

After this event, Anne finds her voice, and Austen represents her conversations as speech rather than reported speech. She becomes aware also of Wentworth's increasing regard and of Mr Elliot's. Whereas in volume I we hear Anne's feelings about her friends and companions through her unspoken thoughts, as volume II progresses she begins to articulate them to her friends. She expresses her feelings about the Musgroves as parents, discusses with Mr Elliot the nature of good company, takes an active part in the later scenes set in the Oval Room and the White Hart in Bath and, finally, takes centre stage in her debate with Captain Harville about the nature of constancy in love.

* * * *

Set against the sterile Elliot dynasty, with its self-obsessed attention to rank and its absence of any useful function, is the naval community. Debrett's *Baronetage of England*, seen to amount to little more than a dictionary of a useless class, contrasts with the navy lists – current lists of ships and their complements – which Anne has used to follow the exploits of Captain Wentworth. The long war against France has just ended and many naval officers have made their fortunes and are looking for a place to settle. Mr Shepherd, Sir Walter's lawyer, sees the economic value of these families and Anne, in one of the few occasions when her direct speech is represented early in the novel, sees their worth in ethical terms:

> The navy, I think, who have done so much for us, have at least an equal claim with any other set of men, for all the comforts and all the privileges which any home can give. Sailors work hard enough for their comforts, we must all allow.
> (Vol. I, Ch. 3)

Admiral Croft, we learn, is a veteran of the famous sea battle of Trafalgar but this information has no effect on Sir Walter. His only concern is that the Admiral will look sunburned, and the fact that his rank in life is inferior to his own will reflect well on himself when he mentions the name to his new acquaintances in Bath.

When we meet the Crofts we encounter a vigorous happy marriage, one of the few successful marriages in all of Austen's fiction. Childless, the Crofts have no foolish ideas of rank and they relate to one another as equals. Mrs Croft asks more questions about the renting of Kellynch than her husband and it is she who takes the reins of the horse to guide their carriage. As his wife and companion she accompanies her husband on many of his sea journeys. They are decisive, making judgments quickly and together, whereas Sir Walter must be persuaded to make all his decisions. Their changes to

Kellynch are sensible practical ones, including removing the mirrors. Anne knows that they will be better caretakers of the great house than was her father:

> ... she had in fact so high an opinion of the Crofts, and considered her father so very fortunate in his tenants, felt the parish to be so sure of a good example, and the poor of the best attention and relief, that however sorry and ashamed for the necessity of the removal, she could not but in conscience feel that they were gone who deserved not to stay, and that Kellynch Hall had passed into better hands than its owners.
>
> (Vol. II, Ch. 1)

For all their lack of rank, the Crofts are kindly people and they feel for Anne on her visit to her old home. They possess a delicacy and sensitivity that the Elliots lack and it is this, their politeness of the heart, that places them higher than Sir Walter in any genealogy of human worth.

Other naval families enter Anne's world. When she meets the Harvilles at Lyme Anne is aware of the loss she has suffered in giving up Captain Wentworth. She might have been a part of this community. The naval families support one another, value comradeship above cosmetics, help out their friends and have no sense of rank. Aware of the frailty of happiness, they try to protect it wherever they can. For this reason, Mrs Croft accompanies her husband on risky sea journeys and Captain Harville takes all the measures he can to get back to his family after a period at sea. Out of regard for others, Wentworth takes care to ensure that the news of the death of Captain Benwick's fiancée reaches him as soon as possible. These close-knit families are set against the world of Bath where there are no real friendships, except through rank, and where an invitation to a home is dependent on a clinical assessment of how much the invitee might improve the social status of the host.

The difference between the naval community and the landed gentry reveals itself in the different attitudes to Dick Musgrove, the never seen son of the Musgrove family who spent some of his misspent youth in the service of Captain Wentworth. He is worthless to everyone and sent to sea by his family as a relief from his presence but Mrs Musgrove weeps over the loss of her son while Captain

Wentworth has more sanguine feelings about him.

> "Poor dear fellow!" continued Mrs Musgrove; "he was grown so steady, and such an excellent correspondent, while he was under your care! Ah! it would have been a happy thing, if he had never left you. I assure you, Captain Wentworth, we are very sorry he ever left you."
>
> There was a momentary expression in Captain Wentworth's face at this speech, a certain glance of his bright eye, and curl of his handsome mouth, which convinced Anne, that instead of sharing in Mrs Musgrove's kind wishes, as to her son, he had probably been at some pains to get rid of him.
>
> (Vol. I, Ch. 8)

The counterpoint of Mrs Musgrove's "large, fat sighings" and her sadness at the loss of a son sounds more like the bitchy Jane Austen of some of her letters than the usual, distant, ironic tone of her novels.

In the portrayal of the naval community we see the marked change which has taken place in Austen's thinking. In this novel, the peerage, far from having a useful role as members of the landed gentry, are regarded as obsolete and redundant and there is a new class which better represents the values that Austen holds dear. This new class of people represent an open, equal society where hard work, skill and the taking of risks are qualities which are a benefit to society. In this new order, rank in itself is unimportant, women can take an equal part in marriages, a few hold down jobs and even engage with men in debate. The peerage owes its position to its ancestors' activities, in some cases to their ancestors' ability to purchase a peerage, while the naval community owes its success to its own efforts.

Captain Frederick Wentworth forms a part of this vibrant, new self-help community. He is also, as heroes go, a new departure for the author. He is headstrong, confident, fearless, brilliant and, at first, spendthrift. Mr Knightley would not approve of his imprudence although he would, one assumes, have approved his forthrightness. He embodies all the good qualities of the naval community but, when we first meet him, he is still headstrong, becoming embroiled with the Musgrove daughters without his even noticing it. He is also still very angry at Anne and our brief trip into his inner thoughts tell us that he is not entirely aware of, or in control of, his feelings towards her:

> He had not forgiven Anne Elliot. She had used him ill, deserted and disappointed him; and worse, she had shewn a feebleness of character in doing so, which his own decided, confident temper could not endure. She had given him up to oblige others. It had been the effect of over-persuasion. It had been weakness and timidity.
>
> He had been most warmly attached to her, and had never seen a woman since whom he thought her equal; but, except from some natural sensation of curiosity, he had no desire of meeting her again. Her power with him was gone for ever.
>
> (Vol. I, Ch. 7)

The gentlemen does, perhaps, protest too much. Anne has had time on her hands to analyse her feelings but Wentworth justifies his without analysis, hence the note of vehemence in his voice that betrays unresolved emotions. It takes just one cathartic moment of physical proximity, when he takes the child from Anne's back, to effect some kind of release for his anger and he is able to act more kindly towards her. It remains for him to learn to appreciate Anne's good qualities. He still believes decisiveness to be of prime importance and when his views on this, expressed to Louisa Musgrove, precipitate the accident at Lyme he finally comes to realize his shortcomings in this regard. When Anne and he are reconciled, they begin a discussion of their past, both recognizing that they might have come together earlier but for his pride. They come to the conclusion that Anne was right to accept Lady Russell's advice to break the engagement but that the advice was wrong in the first place. In many ways, this novel replays the themes of *Sense and Sensibility* but concludes this time more equitably between the two ideas. Anne has learned to be less sensible and Wentworth less passionate.

Lady Russell, however good intentioned, is another example of the barrenness of her class. Long before Sir Walter is forced to become a transient figure, she spends her time in travel and like other members of her class, she is shiftless. Lady Russell has perfect manners and considerable insight. She can see the inappropriateness of Mrs Clay's friendship with Elizabeth and her father and she loves Anne and wishes her to be more important in her own family circle. Despite these insights, she is essentially a member of a moribund class, unable to change her opinions and unwilling to accept the elements of risk and change that Captain Wentworth represents. She fears that a marriage to such a "nobody" would be a waste of Anne's youth and beauty but, instead, it has been her advice which destroyed Anne's bloom.

In *Emma*, the story moves seamlessly through the rather boring daily events of a village community. It is entirely likely that a group of friends should pick strawberries, hold dinner parties or take a day trip to Box Hill. In *Persuasion*, as in *Pride and Prejudice*, we see a return to the use of fortuitous events as the plot works to bring the two main characters together, thus furthering their reconciliation. So, we have Mr Elliot happening to stay at the same inn as Anne, Louisa's accident, the Crofts taking Kellynch, and Anne's friend being involved with Mr Elliot and having information about him through Nurse Rooke. It is possible, had she lived longer, that Jane Austen might have tidied up this fairly short novel, some parts of which seem sketchy.

Mr Elliot is a case in point. There is no reason for him to be introduced at Lyme because he could easily have been brought into the story in Bath. In the love story of Anne and Frederick he is a side note; briefly considered for his fine manners and sensibilities but rejected long before Mrs Smith's revelations about him. Captain Wentworth has begun to love Anne again and his jealousy over Anne and her cousin is unfounded. Even Mr Elliot's scheming with Mrs Clay is unnecessary because, in a way, who cares what happens to Kellynch?

Mrs Smith too represents a plot device, with a whole chapter of exposition which the author of *Emma*, in a better state of health, might have woven more easily into the plot. Mrs Smith represents the women of earlier novels and, like Jane Fairfax, she is at the mercy of men and her future is only made secure by the forthright intervention of Wentworth, a member of the new society. But there are some very different women in this novel. There is Mrs Croft, Anne's mother, who managed her husband and his estate well until her death, and Mrs Harville who nurses Louisa. Nurse Rooke is an independent woman, as of course is Anne herself and we know she will form an equal and happy union with Wentworth.

Austen's concern with relations between men and women is played out in the final set piece in the White Hart in Bath. Most of Anne's good friends are there and while Captain Wentworth is occupied across the room, apparently engaged in writing a letter, and after Mrs Musgrove and Mrs Croft have discussed the advisability of long engagements, she discusses with Captain Harville the nature of men and women and their feelings for one another. Anne has found her voice. She is no longer prudent and silent and she expresses her ideas about the nature of love. The conversation begins over the miniature portrait Captain Benwick had commissioned for Harville's sister but which he now prepares for his new fiancée Louisa. Harville declares that his sister would not have forgotten Benwick so quickly as he has forgotten her. Anne takes up the point, insisting that all women would maintain their love for longer than men, since they have no occupation and because it is in their nature to love when all hope is lost. Seemingly talking generalities, Anne is really talking about her own sense of loss and mourning and she becomes more roused, coherent and assertive as she proceeds. After Anne has passionately asserted women's deeper feelings and Harville calls on literature and history to prove men to be the more constant in love, Anne replies for all women:

> Yes, yes, if you please, no reference to examples in books. Men have had every advantage of us in telling their own story. Education has been theirs in so much higher a degree; the pen has been in their hands. I will not allow books to prove anything.
>
> (Vol. III, Ch. 11)

As they talk, Wentworth's pen falls – he has clearly been listening and has for the moment been overcome by her words – the pen has left his hands. By the end of the conversation, Anne is almost too moved to speak. This scene, rather than the ones that follow, is the emotional climax of the novel. Anne has learned to bring her abilities together in a consummate manner, articulating her feelings while confidently expressing herself as a physical creature. Harville is moved by her words to touch her arm, to make physical contact with someone who for a long time has not registered with others as an independent individual. Listening to her articulate her feelings so eloquently has given Wentworth the impetus he needs to make the reconciliation. In this way, it is Anne's words and her ability to express her feelings that allows Wentworth to declare himself and, in this way, she is the heroine of her own story – something that none of the other heroines managed to achieve.

7

Last Words

> "You will find Captain ... a very respectable, well meaning man, without much manner, his wife and sister all good humour and obligingness, and I hope (since the fashion allows it) with rather longer petticoats than last year."
>
> (Jane Austen's last written words, in a letter to a friend.)

Sanditon

Written between 17th January and 18th March 1817, *Sanditon* is a 22,000-word fragment, barely sketched out in places, that represents a radical departure in style, subject matter and tone from Austen's earlier novels. The landed gentry, living in and rarely departing from their own milieu, are no longer her concern, nor is their stable, unchanging environment. Whereas the other novels begin with a statement regarding the social and economic status of the family in question, this one begins with an unnamed man and woman travelling in unknown territory, in a hired carriage along lanes unsuitable for them, in search of an unknown goal. Here we are in Regency England, with all the upheaval that Austen saw in the post-war years foregrounding the latest story she has to tell.

Mr Parker, the traveller, is a business man and the business he is undertaking is the creation of an entirely new community, a seaside resort dedicated to the new fashion of health. His business is as risky as his carriage journey and takes up the theme of transience and restlessness evident in *Persuasion*. His journey, unlike his obsession with the new town, ends fortuitously, for although his carriage is overturned and his ankle injured he and his wife meet the Heywood family, a vestige of Austen's old England. Mr Heywood is in his fields making hay alongside his estate workers, taking care of, and earning respect from, those whose livelihoods depend on his good management of the estate. The Heywoods are stability personified, rarely leaving home, uninterested in new-fangled carriages or ideas, conserving their finances to support a huge family, happy in a small circle of friends but prepared to sacrifice their own needs for their children to travel away from home. The Heywoods quickly pass out of our sight, an anachronism in a Regency England where large numbers of demobilised sailors and soldiers have come home with no work to take up and where new inventions are changing English life forever. The inflating economy encourages new investments from a new class of entrepreneurs, some of whom respond to the demands of a gentry, seen in *Persuasion* in the form of Lady Russell and Sir Walter, who now prefer popular resorts to the quiet of their own homes.

One of the sensible Heywood daughters accompanies the Parkers back to Sanditon and provides Austen with a willing pair of discriminating eyes. We see the foolish activities which Parker believes to be improvements. The new home he has built has no shade-providing trees, unlike the old house he has let out. The terraces of empty houses and the fancy shoes being sold in what was once a simple village shoemaker's are testimony to the hollow worth of his endeavours. Parker and his partner, the avaricious Lady Denham, calculate the exact value of each family that arrives, accepting that more people will put prices up so they can increase their rents.

Parker's brother and sisters arrive, introducing another of Austen's themes, the culture of ill health. Two very healthy women and an overweight, lazy brother join the social circle, the elder sister having many of the traits already seen to cause trouble in the other novels, in particular her tendency to interfere in the lives of others. This propensity to interfere is taken to a ridiculous extreme in her arrangements on behalf of two groups of visitors, neither of which she has ever met and who turn out to be the one group after all.

The other characters in *Sanditon* are a foolish young man who has misread romantic fiction and imagines himself a seducer, a penniless but beautiful female companion to Lady Denham and a wealthy mulatto girl. Sadly, Austen never had time to get any further. The tone of this novel returns towards *Northanger Abbey* in respect of its humour, almost burlesque at times, and its heroine seems as sensible as Catherine but in no way endowed with her naivety. The shift in the focus of Austen's writing, from a stable, small village community that is ultimately approved of despite its shortcomings, to *Sanditon*'s shiftless, cash-fixated individuals, is dramatic. The fragment that we have evokes a debilitating, non-community of hypochondriacs and members of the landed gentry whose only object in life is to squeeze as much cash as possible out of their customers. This marks a remarkable change in Austen's outlook, though one that can be seen to be developing in *Persuasion*, and it indicates a new kind of critical awareness of the changes taking place in her society. In *Sanditon*, her rootless characters are on the move and the author's old world of stable values is fading from the scene.

Language and Style

The humour in Austen's novels, lying not only in the amusing events and colourful characters in her books, can be seen in the way she takes the language of the fiction written before her and creates something altogether more subtle and innovative. Sir Walter Scott, in an anonymous review of his own early novels, was able to see how his male characters were "all brethren of a family; very amiable and very insipid sort of young men" (*Quarterly Review* 16, 1817). Austen is far more successful in avoiding this tendency and, although her characterisation of Darcy, her first attempt at a hero, is weak, her own heroines and heroes mostly develop their own distinctive styles of speaking and thinking.

One way of distinguishing the worth of a character is to look at their use of figurative language. In the passages which represent the observing, omniscient narrator, metaphor is rarely used and Austen clearly suspected its use. On the few occasions when the narrator uses metaphor it is ironic: "And now I may dismiss my heroine to the sleepless couch, which is the true heroine's portion; to a pillow strewed with thorns and wet with tears." (*Northanger Abbey*, Vol. I, Ch. 12). Where figurative language is used, it tends to be found in the speech of the more foolish characters. Mr Collins offers "an olive branch", Mary Bennet feels the need to "stem the tide of malice and pour into the wounded bosoms of each other the balm of sisterly consolation", Lady Catherine asks "are the shades of Pemberly to be thus polluted?" and Mrs Elton smirkingly refers to "Hymen's saffron robe". The figurative clichés boost the self-image of the person using them and, by calling on familiar moral sound-bites to bolster their unoriginal opinions, give them (and only them, for no one else is fooled) a feeling of moral soundness.

Another technique perfected by Austen, the use of free indirect speech, allows the reader to hear the conversations and detect the attitudes of her characters, while being aware of standing outside of them, listening in. What we read, mediated by the author, is the language the character would use if they were speaking. Austen both mimics their speech and distances herself, and us, from it. It is a form of irony and, given the distinctive and often self-deluding ways they have of speaking, is one of the ways in which Austen brings a character to life. For example, consider the single use of irony at Fanny's expense in *Mansfield Park*. Fanny is watching Edmund give a riding lesson to Mary Crawford:

> After a few minutes they stopped entirely. Edmund was close to her; he was speaking to her; he was evidently directing her management of the bridle; he had hold of her hand; she saw it, or the imagination supplied what the eye could not reach. She must not wonder at all this; what could be more natural than that Edmund should be making himself useful, and proving his good-nature by any one? She could not but think, indeed, that Mr Crawford might as well have saved him the trouble; that it would have been particularly proper and becoming in a brother to have done it himself; but Mr Crawford, with all his boasted good-nature, and all his coachmanship, probably knew nothing of the matter, and had no active kindness in comparison of Edmund. She began to think it rather hard upon the mare to have such double duty; if she were forgotten, the poor mare should be remembered.
> (Vol. I, Ch. 6)

The tone of Fanny's inner thoughts are characteristically hers. Any of the other cousins would express their feelings more colourfully but here Fanny's mild character determines the tone. Fanny is annoyed and jealous and full of self-pity. She has been forgotten, Miss Crawford is a far better rider than she is, the man she loves is paying attention to this lively, attractive other woman. Fanny can't accept these feelings but neither is she able to feel annoyed at Edmund, so they are translated into seeing what others might consider the physical attraction between the two riders into approval of Edmund's kindness, contempt for Mr Crawford and pity for the horse. As she sees Edmund take Mary Crawford's hand (or at least imagines she sees it) we hear "she must not wonder at all this ..." We hear the proper young lady telling herself that her feelings of 'wonder' are wrong. Then "She could not but think ..." instead of a simpler 'she thought'. Fanny is unused to having strong opinions about her cousin's Edmund's behaviour and so she must couch her feelings in double negatives, reducing their impact. The author and the reader laugh quietly together at the forgivably tiny act of self-delusion on Fanny's part.

In *Emma*, this free indirect speech forms the heart of the novel. We see events through Emma's eyes, hear her inner thoughts and are aware of every time she justifies her actions to herself or makes a adjustment, to suit her needs, to what she knows to be the proper way of behaving. A good example of this is when Emma, at Mr Cole's house, observes Harriet and Jane Fairfax:

> Emma watched the entry of her own particular little friend; and if she could not exult in her dignity and grace, she could not only love the blooming sweetness and the artless manner, but could most heartily rejoice in that light, cheerful, unsentimental disposition which allowed her so many alleviations of pleasure, in the midst of the pangs of disappointed affection. There she sat – and who would have guessed how many tears she had been lately shedding? To be in company, nicely dressed herself and seeing others nicely dressed, to sit and smile and look pretty, and say nothing, was enough for the happiness of the present hour. Jane Fairfax did look and move superior; but Emma suspected she might have been glad to change feelings with Harriet, very glad to have purchased the mortification of having loved – yes, of having loved even Mr Elton in vain – by the surrender of all the dangerous pleasure of knowing herself beloved by the husband of her friend.
>
> (Vol. II, Ch. 26)

The passage looks first at Harriet through Emma's eyes, seeing what she chooses to see. Months have passed since Harriet's disappointment over Mr Elton, she has reformed her friendship with the Martins and had a friendly conversation with Robert Martin. In fact, Emma has had to distract her from Robert Martin by reminding her of Mr Elton's marriage. Emma cannot in all honesty make the simple Harriet into a tragic figure but she does her best with "in the midst of the pangs of disappointed affection". Harriet, though, is not able to sustain Emma's interest for long and she turns her attention to Jane Fairfax, for whom she has invented another story – that she has had a love affair with her friend's husband. Her thoughts take on the overtones of rhetoric with "having loved – yes, of having loved even Mr Elton ..." and "by the surrender of all the dangerous pleasure ..." The reader can almost hear Emma making up the lurid story using the language of the romance novel. This disparity between what Emma wants to believe and the reality makes up the humour of the novel and helps turn a rather selfish, self-deluded heroine into someone whom, while recognising her faults, we can find endearing.

Sometimes, a character is so lacking in subtlety that the use of free, indirect speech is unnecessary and in this respect Mr Collins is a rich and wonderful source for Austen's use of irony. Here he is asking Elizabeth to marry him:

> My reasons for marrying are, first, that I think it a right thing for every clergyman in easy circumstances (like myself) to set the example of matrimony in his parish; secondly, that I am convinced that it will add very greatly to my happiness; and thirdly – which perhaps I ought to have mentioned earlier, that it is the particular advice and recommendation of the very noble lady whom I have the honour of calling patroness.

Mr Collins' rhetorical beginning is laughable. First, he reminds Elizabeth of his importance and financial status and his moral obligation to encourage his parishioners to marry – as if they might fail to think of marrying without his example. Then, and only secondly, he thinks he will be happier married, couching the thought in a rather pompous way ("add very greatly to my happiness"). It does not occur to him to say something about why Elizabeth will make him happy. The third, most spurious reason is that Lady Catherine told him to marry and his own conceit is mirrored in the florid, self-important language that he uses to describe her ("the very noble lady whom I have the honour of calling patroness").

He goes on:

> Twice has she condescended to give me her opinion (unasked too!) on this subject; and it was but the very Saturday night before I left Hunsford – between our pools at quadrille, while Mrs Jenkinson was arranging Miss de Bourgh's footstool, that she said, "Mr Collins, you must marry. A clergyman like you must marry. Choose properly, choose a gentlewoman for *my* sake; and for your *own*, let her be an active, useful sort of person, not brought up high, but able to make a small income go a good way. This is my advice. Find such a woman as soon as you can, bring her to Hunsford, and I will visit her."

The rhetoric continues with the phrasing and tone of a rehearsed speech (he later tells Elizabeth that he practises what to say to Lady Catherine), and he cannot help but slip in some delightful and, he mistakenly believes, impressive details of his superior social life at Hunsford. The next sentiment he expresses contains Lady Catherine's instructions for the type of wife he is to choose. He utterly fails to be aware of how insulting it must be to Elizabeth to hear his shopping list of requirements in a wife, the principal one being that she must have entertainment value for Lady Catherine. If there were any chance of Elizabeth marrying him before he began, there certainly is not now. He assumes at all times that his ideas of the condescension of Lady Catherine are universal ones and has no idea that what he says might be offensive. The footstool detail, with its broken phrase inserted into his sentence, suggests that his mind wanders back to the honour of being in such great company and suggests his belief that his foolish, obsequious, self-important life must be interesting to this woman.

There is more:

> Allow me, by the way, to observe, my fair cousin, that I do not reckon the notice and kindness of Lady Catherine de Bourgh as among the least of the advantages in my power to offer. You will find her manners beyond anything I can describe; and your wit and vivacity, I think, must be acceptable to her, especially when tempered with the silence and respect which her rank will inevitably excite.

A modest reprimand to Elizabeth. He quietly suggests that when she is presented to Lady Catherine she keeps silent, couched in what he imagines to be gentle, courteous language ("especially when tempered with ..."). Mr Collins is laying out the life that the grateful Elizabeth can expect, the chief advantage of which is the proximity of the great lady. His language – the language Austen provides for him – constitutes the pomposity and obsequiousness of the man. At no point does his language become too silly to believe and the reader, along with Elizabeth, stands amazed as the man blindly exposes his follies.

> Thus much for my general intention in favour of matrimony; it remains to be told why my views were directed towards Longbourn instead of my own neighbourhood, where I can assure you there are many amiable young women. But the fact is, that being, as I am, to inherit this estate after the death of your honoured father (who, however, may live many years longer), I could not satisfy myself without resolving to choose a wife from among his daughters, that the loss to them might be as little as possible, when the melancholy event takes place – which, however, as I have already said, may not be for several years.

Here we see Mr Collins imagining himself to be the master of good taste when he refers to her father's death, which he is careful to point out, twice, may not be for a very long time. The fact that he mentions it at all in a marriage proposal shows his inability to experience any real feeling for Elizabeth. In one way, his choosing a wife from among Mr Bennet's daughters is a kindly action, since they do not have much in the way of a dowry and he will be taking their home away when their father dies, but the fact that he tells Elizabeth of his generosity and assumes her gratitude makes it offensive:

> This has been my motive, my fair cousin, and I flatter myself it will not sink me in your esteem. And now nothing remains for me but to assure you in the most animated language of the violence of my affection. To fortune I am perfectly indifferent, and shall make no demand of that nature on your father, since I am well aware that it could not be complied with; and that one thousand pounds in the four per cents, which will not be yours till after your mother's decease, is all that you may ever

> be entitled to. On that head, therefore, I shall be uniformly silent; and you may assure yourself that no ungenerous reproach shall ever pass my lips when we are married.

The delusion continues, with the flourish of "my fair cousin" and, ironically speaking quite truthfully, "I flatter myself". He adds an assurance that he will never remind her of her debt to him, although he is already doing just that, while at the same time pointing out that he has already discovered what she will bring to the marriage ("one thousand in the four per cents"). The complete lack of any feeling in his speech is amplified by his conclusion. He has laid out his shopping list of needs, said what he has to offer, and is unable to actually put any feeling into his words so he tells her what he is telling her: "nothing remains for me but to assure you in the most animated language of the violence of my affection". This is all a little like Austen telling us what to think about Eleanor's husband in *Northanger Abbey*: "Any further definition of his merits must be unnecessary; the most charming young man in the world is instantly before the imagination of us all." (Vol. II, Ch. 16). In *Northanger Abbey* this instruction to the reader to understand certain ideas without the author taking the trouble to display them through character or event is by a wry, amused narrator; here it is by someone about as un-omniscient as is possible. A lesser writer might tell us what a pompous creature Mr Collins is by way of an authorial intrusion but Austen allows Mr Collins' language – his clichés, crass remarks and tone of both servility and pompousness – to speak for itself. How much of this speech he recycles when he proposes to Charlotte Lucas we will never know but with Elizabeth's good friend his language has the effect he desires. Or perhaps, to give Charlotte some intelligence, she is able and willing to screen out his use of language because of her own reasons for wishing to marry.

In *Mansfield Park*, the language has become more subtle and the irony harder to identify but characters still give themselves away. Here is Henry Crawford talking to his sister about Fanny:

> "I will not do her any harm, dear little soul! only want her to look kindly on me, to give me smiles as well as blushes, to keep a chair for me by herself wherever we are, and be all animation when I take it and talk to her; to think as I think, be

interested in all my possessions and pleasures, try to keep me
longer at Mansfield, and feel when I go away that she shall be
never happy again. I want nothing more."

(Vol. II, Ch. 24)

What he wants to do, basically, is crush her, make her love him and then walk away when he has done so. His callous intentions are told in a light-hearted tone, as if it were just a bit of fun he is proposing, not the breaking of a young girl's heart. The light-heartedness of the tone, together with the affectionate "dear little soul" makes the conversation all the more chilling. The speech is characteristically Henry's, containing 11 references to himself. The first long sentence flows with the confidence of the character and the long list of wants is followed by the simple "I want nothing more", that is he wants everything.

Austen's style moves smoothly between simple narrative, authorial interventions and devastating character assassinations, with the occasional acerbic comment on life: "… a few clever things said, a few downright silly, but by much the larger proportion neither the one nor the other – nothing worse than everyday remarks, dull repetitions, old news, and heavy jokes." (*Emma*, Vol. II, Ch. 7). Her characters have distinctive, natural voices, from the apparent chaos of Miss Bates' train of thought to the decisive, affirmative tones of Mr Knightley or Frederick Wentworth and each, through Austen's innovative invention of free indirect speech, reveals themselves in subtle and often deliciously funny ways.

In conclusion, one can say that, like the characters travelling in the opening lines of *Sanditon*, Austen's fiction has made an eventful journey of its own. Her novels have moved from the fantasy romance of *Pride and Prejudice* with its remote but mindful landowner and his lively new wife, through the moral decay and recuperation of *Mansfield Park* and the rejection of that class in *Persuasion*, to a final, tantalising suggestion in *Sanditon* of how the author, now in her forties, was sardonically viewing the world. Taken as a whole, Austen's novels refute the criticism that is still sometimes made of her, namely that she is essentially a miniaturist, a novelist of limited experience and therefore of limited interest. She may not openly engage with political and social issues but her engagement with the values of her society is a deep and critical one. In 1942, the philosopher Georges Friedman, in *La Puissance de la sagese,* wrote about the need to acquire a personal sense of worth and he saw it as just as vital, if not more so, as more public issues of a political kind:

> Every day a 'spiritual exercise' alone or in the company of a man who wishes to better himself ... Leave ordinary time behind. Make an effort to rid yourself of your own passions ... Become eternal by surpassing yourself. This inner effort is necessary, this ambition, just. Many are those who are entirely absorbed in militant politics, in the preparation for the social revolution. Rare, very rare, are those who, in order to prepare for the revolution, wish to become worthy of it.

Jane Austen was not seeking to prepare for a revolution but she was acutely concerned with the need to better oneself and become worthy through a self-learning process of coming to know oneself. The happiness that does eventually come to those Austen heroines that most readers admire, arises very much through the kind of "inner effort" that Friedman has in mind. The changes for the good that are undergone by Austen's characters do not come about easily and certainly not through some accident of the plot. They arise through a process of reasoning and self-reflection, a willingness to learn and admit mistakes, and the novels are all about this learning process. They are not about young women finding husbands but about the importance of becoming worthy.

Bibliography

Texts

Both the Everyman Library and Penguin Classics editions of the novels are excellent, with illuminating introductions and useful notes on the text. One of the Penguin Classics collects together *Lady Susan*, *The Watsons* and *Sanditon*, with some explanatory notes. Online, the Project Gutenberg Etexts (www.gutenberg.org) are indispensable for searching the texts. There is no online version of *Sanditon*. Hesperus Press publishes several of the juvenilia including *Lesley Castle*, *The Watsons*, *Love and Friendship* and *Lady Susan* as single volumes. *Jane Austen Selected Letters* is published by Oxford World Classics.

Penguin publishes abridged recordings of the novels on CD (www.penguinclassics.co.uk) and Naxos (www.naxos.com) publish abridged and unabridged recordings of the novels.

The BBC has made available (BBC DVD 1748) a collection of television adaptations of the novels including the famous Darcy-taking-a-swim version of *Pride and Prejudice* of 1995. Other productions date back to the 1980s with a 1972 version of *Emma* which shows its age but has a brittle, perpetually smiling Emma and a wonderful Mrs Elton. *Sense and Sensibility* is the finest of the collection.

The Oneworld Classics series (www.oneworldclassics.com) includes two Jane Austen novels, *Pride and Prejudice* and *Emma*, and they are the kind of lovely books that you would want to keep as well as read. Affordably priced, they come with a useful critical apparatus – including illustrations and a section on the life and work of the author – and, best of all, they are produced using quality paper, sewn binding and a high regard for the typographical values of a book. Hopefully, more Austen titles will appear in this laudable series.

Biographies

A Memoir of Jane Austen, J.E. Austen-Leigh (OUP, 2002). Jane Austen's Life and Times, written by her nephew.
Jane Austen: A Life, Claire Tomalin (Penguin, 1997). A study of the minutiae of Austen's life and works which draws a distinct character from the known facts of her life, her letters and her prose works.
Jane Austen, Carol Shields (Phoenix, 2001). A study of Austen's life which also looks closely at the novels.

Critical and background reading

A Fine Brush on Ivory, Richard Jenkyns (Oxford, 2004). Quirky but insightful views on the novels.
Critical Essays on Jane Austen, ed. B.C. Southam (Routledge, 1970). Classic Austen criticism.
Critical Issues: Jane Austen, Darryl Jones (Palgrave, 2004). Modern critical theory and lots of historical background.
Culture and Imperialism, Edward Said (Vintage, 1994). Contains an excellent study of *Mansfield Park*.
Emma: Character and Construction, Edgar F. Shannon Jr. (1956) debates Mudrick's view of the novel.
Irony as Form, Marvin Mudrick (1952). A study of *Emma*, suggesting an interesting and alternative reading of the heroine.
Jane Austen and the Morality of Conversation, Bharat Tandon (Anthem, 2003). Focuses on style, particularly free indirect speech.
Jane Austen, Mansfield Park: A Reader's Guide to Essential Criticism, ed. Sandie Byrne (Palgrave, 2005). Outline of studies of the novel from its publication to the present.
Jane Austen: Real and Imagined Worlds, Oliver MacDonagh (Yale University Press, 1991). Useful studies of Austen's works including *Sanditon*.
Jane Austen: The World of Her Novels, Deirdre le Faye (Frances Lincoln, 2002). Excellent background reading on the places that Jane Austen lived in and wrote about as well as studies of the novels.
Jane Austen, or the Secret of Style, D.A. Miller (Princeton, 2003). Studies, among other aspects, the style of the omniscient narrator.
Jane Austen, Tony Tanner (Macmillan, 1986). Definitive study of the novels showing a process of change in Austen's attitude to society

through the course of her life.

Jane Austen's Novels: A Study in Structure, Andrew H. Wright (Penguin, 1962). Studies of the main characters and a chapter on Jane Austen's stylistic techniques.

Romancing Jane Austen, Ashley Tauchert (Palgrave, 2005). A study of Austen and the romance novel.

So You Think You Know Jane Austen, John Sutherland and Deirdre le Faye (Oxford, 2005). Fun-filled pages of increasingly difficult quizzes on the novels.

The Cambridge Companion to Jane Austen, eds. Edward Copeland and Juliet McMaster (Cambridge, 1997). A collection of essays which put Austen into her historical and social context.

The Gentleman's Daughter: Women's Lives in Georgian England, Amanda Vickery (Yale, 1998). A study of women of Austen's class and time, which illustrates just how much of a fantasy the marriage of Elizabeth and Darcy was.

GREENWICH EXCHANGE BOOKS

STUDENT GUIDE LITERARY SERIES

The Greenwich Exchange Student Guide Literary Series is a collection of critical essays of major or contemporary serious writers in English and selected European languages. The series is for the student, the teacher and 'common readers' and is an ideal resource for libraries. The *Times Educational Supplement* praised these books, saying, "The style of [this series] has a pressure of meaning behind it. Readers should learn from that ... If art is about selection, perception and taste, then this is it."

(ISBN prefix 978-1-871551 applies unless marked* when 978-1-906075 applies).
All books are paperbacks unless otherwise stated.

The series includes:
W.H. Auden by Stephen Wade (36-5)
Jane Austen by Paty Levy (89-1)
Antonin Artaud by Lee Jamieson (98-3)
Honoré de Balzac by Wendy Mercer (48-8)
William Blake by Peter Davies (27-3)
The Brontës by Peter Davies (24-2)
Robert Browning by John Lucas (59-4)
Lord Byron by Andrew Keanie (83-9)
Samuel Taylor Coleridge by Andrew Keanie (64-8)
Joseph Conrad by Martin Seymour-Smith (18-1)
William Cowper by Michael Thorn (25-9)
Charles Dickens by Robert Giddings (26-9)
Emily Dickinson by Marnie Pomeroy (68-6)
John Donne by Sean Haldane (23-5)
Ford Madox Ford by Anthony Fowles (63-1)
The Stagecraft of Brian Friel by David Grant (74-7)
Robert Frost by Warren Hope (70-9)
Patrick Hamilton by John Harding (99-0)
Thomas Hardy by Sean Haldane (33-4)
Seamus Heaney by Warren Hope (37-2)
Joseph Heller by Anthony Fowles (84-6)
Gerard Manley Hopkins by Sean Sheehan (77-3)
James Joyce by Michael Murphy (73-0)
Philip Larkin by Warren Hope (35-8)

Laughter in the Dark – The Plays of Joe Orton by Arthur Burke (56-3)
Sylvia Plath by Marnie Pomeroy (88-4)
George Orwell by Warren Hope (42-6)
Poets of the First World War by John Greening (79-2)
Philip Roth by Paul McDonald (72-3)
Shakespeare's *A Midsummer Night's Dream* by Matt Simpson (90-7)
Shakespeare's *Hamlet* by Peter Davies (12-5)*
Shakespeare's *King Lear* by Peter Davies (95-2)
Shakespeare's *Macbeth* by Matt Simpson (69-3)
Shakespeare's *Much Ado About Nothing* by Matt Simpson (01-9)*
Shakespeare's *Othello* by Matt Simpson (71-5)
Shakespeare's Second Tetralogy: *Richard II – Henry V* by John Lucas (97-6)
Shakespeare's *The Merchant of Venice* by Alan Ablewhite (96-9)
Shakespeare's *The Tempest* by Matt Simpson (75-4)
Shakespeare's *Twelfth Night* by Matt Simpson (86-0)
Shakespeare's *The Winter's Tale* by John Lucas (80-3)
Shakespeare's Non-Dramatic Poetry by Martin Seymour-Smith (22-6)
Shakespeare's Sonnets by Martin Seymour-Smith (38-9)
Tobias Smollett by Robert Giddings (21-1)
Dylan Thomas by Peter Davies (78-5)
Alfred, Lord Tennyson by Michael Thorn (20-4)
William Wordsworth by Andrew Keanie (57-0)
W.B. Yeats by John Greening (34-1)

FOCUS ON SERIES

Emily Brontë's *Wuthering Heights* by Matt Simpson (10-1)*
George Eliot's *Middlemarch* by John Axon (06-4)*
T.S. Eliot's *The Waste Land* by Matt Simpson (09-5)*
Michael Frayn's *Spies* by Angela Topping (08-8)*
Thomas Hardy: *Poems of 1912–13* by John Greening (04-0)*
The Poetry of Ted Hughes by John Greening (05-7)*
The Poetry of Tony Harrison by Sean Sheehan (15.6)*
James Joyce's *A Portrait of the Artist as a Young Man* by
   Matt Simpson (07-1)*
Harold Pinter by Lee Jamieson (16-3)*

LITERATURE & BIOGRAPHY

Matthew Arnold and 'Thyrsis' *by Patrick Carill Connolly*
Matthew Arnold (1822-1888) was a leading poet, intellect and aesthete of the Victorian epoch. He is now best known for his strictures as a literary

and cultural critic, and educationist. After a long period of neglect, his views have come in for a revaluation. Arnold's poetry remains less well known, yet his poems and his understanding of poetry, which defied the conventions of his time, were central to his achievement.

The author traces Arnold's intellectual and poetic development, showing how his poetry gathers its meanings from a lifetime's study of European literature and philosophy. Connolly's unique exegesis of 'Thyrsis' draws upon a wide-ranging analysis of the pastoral and its associated myths in both classical and native cultures. This study shows lucidly and in detail how Arnold encouraged the intense reflection of the mind on the subject placed before it, believing in " ... the all importance of the choice of the subject, the necessity of accurate observation; and subordinate character of expression."

Patrick Carill Connolly gained his English degree at Reading University and taught English literature abroad for a number of years before returning to Britain. He is now a civil servant living in London.

2004 • 180 pages • ISBN 978-1-871551-61-7

The Author, the Book and the Reader *by Robert Giddings*
This collection of essays analyses the effects of changing technology and the attendant commercial pressures on literary styles and subject matter. Authors covered include Charles Dickens, Tobias Smollett, Mark Twain, Dr Johnson and John le Carré.
1991 • 220 pages • illustrated • ISBN 978-1-871551-01-3

Norman Cameron *by Warren Hope*
Cameron's poetry was admired by Auden; celebrated by Dylan Thomas; valued by Robert Graves. He was described by Martin Seymour-Smith as "one of ... the most rewarding and pure poets of his generation ..." and is at last given a full-length biography. This eminently sociable man, who had periods of darkness and despair, wrote little poetry by comparison with others of his time, but always of a consistently high quality – imaginative and profound.

Warren Hope is a poet, a critic and university lecturer. He lives and works in Philadelphia, where he raised his family.
2000 • 226 pages • ISBN 978-1-871551-05-1

Aleister Crowley and the Cult of Pan *by Paul Newman*
Few more nightmarish figures stalk English literature than Aleister Crowley (1875-1947), poet, magician, mountaineer and agent provocateur. In this groundbreaking study, Paul Newman dives into the occult mire of Crowley's works and fishes out gems and grotesqueries that are by turns ethereal, sublime, pornographic and horrifying. Like Oscar Wilde before him,

Crowley stood in "symbolic relationship to his age" and to contemporaries like Rupert Brooke, G.K. Chesterton and the Portuguese modernist, Fernando Pessoa. An influential exponent of the cult of the Great God Pan, his essentially 'pagan' outlook was shared by major European writers as well as English novelists like E.M. Forster, D.H. Lawrence and Arthur Machen.

Paul Newman lives in Cornwall. Editor of the literary magazine *Abraxas*, he has written over ten books.

2004 • 222 pages • ISBN 978-1-871551-66-2

John Dryden *by Anthony Fowles*

Of all the poets of the Augustan age, John Dryden was the most worldly. Anthony Fowles traces Dryden's evolution from 'wordsmith' to major poet. This critical study shows a poet of vigour and technical panache whose art was forged in the heat and battle of a turbulent polemical and pamphleteering age. Although Dryden's status as a literary critic has long been established, Fowles draws attention to his neglected achievements as a translator of poetry. He deals also with the less well-known aspects of Dryden's work – his plays and occasional pieces.

Born in London and educated at the Universities of Oxford and Southern California, Anthony Fowles began his career in film-making before becoming an author of film and television scripts and more than twenty books. Readers will welcome the many contemporary references to novels and film with which Fowles illuminates the life and work of this decisively influential English poetic voice.

2003 • 292 pages • ISBN 978-1-871551-58-7

The Good That We Do *by John Lucas*

John Lucas' book blends fiction, biography and social history in order to tell the story of his grandfather, Horace Kelly. Headteacher of a succession of elementary schools in impoverished areas of London, 'Hod' Kelly was also a keen cricketer, a devotee of the music hall, and included among his friends the great trade union leader Ernest Bevin. In telling the story of his life, Lucas has provided a fascinating range of insights into the lives of ordinary Londoners from the First World War until the outbreak of the Second World War. Threaded throughout is an account of such people's hunger for education, and of the different ways government, church and educational officialdom ministered to that hunger. *The Good That We Do* is both a study of one man and of a period when England changed, drastically and forever.

John Lucas is Professor Emeritus of the Universities of Loughborough and Nottingham Trent. He is the author of numerous works of a critical and

scholarly nature and has published eight collections of poetry.
2001 • 214 pages • ISBN 978-1-871551-54-9

D.H. Lawrence: The Nomadic Years, 1919-1930 *by Philip Callow*
This book provides a fresh insight into Lawrence's art as well as his life. Candid about the relationship between Lawrence and his wife, it shows nevertheless the strength of the bond between them. If no other book persuaded the reader of Lawrence's greatness, this does.
Philip Callow was born in Birmingham and studied engineering and teaching before he turned to writing. He has published 14 novels, several collections of short stories and poems, a volume of autobiography, and biographies on the lives of Chekhov, Cezanne, Robert Louis Stevenson, Walt Whitman and Van Gogh all of which have received critical acclaim. His biography of D.H. Lawrence's early years, *Son and Lover*, was widely praised.
2006 • 226 pages • ISBN 978-1-871551-82-2

Liar! Liar!: Jack Kerouac – Novelist *by R.J. Ellis*
The fullest study of Jack Kerouac's fiction to date. It is the first book to devote an individual chapter to every one of his novels. *On the Road*, *Visions of Cody* and *The Subterraneans* are reread in-depth, in a new and exciting way. *Visions of Gerard* and *Doctor Sax* are also strikingly reinterpreted, as are other daringly innovative writings, like 'The Railroad Earth' and his "try at a spontaneous *Finnegans Wake*" – *Old Angel Midnight*. Neglected writings, such as *Tristessa* and *Big Sur*, are also analysed, alongside better-known novels such as *Dharma Bums* and *Desolation Angels*.
R.J. Ellis is Senior Lecturer in English at Nottingham Trent University.
1999 • 294 pages • ISBN 978-1-871551-53-2

Musical Offering *by Yolanthe Leigh*
In a series of vivid sketches, anecdotes and reflections, Yolanthe Leigh tells the story of her growing up in the Poland of the 1930s and the Second World War. These are poignant episodes of a child's first encounters with both the enchantments and the cruelties of the world; and from a later time, stark memories of the brutality of the Nazi invasion, and the hardships of student life in Warsaw under the Occupation. But most of all this is a record of inward development; passages of remarkable intensity and simplicity describe the girl's response to religion, to music, and to her discovery of philosophy.
Yolanthe Leigh was formerly a Lecturer in Philosophy at Reading University.
2000 • 56 pages • ISBN: 978-1-871551-46-4

In Pursuit of Lewis Carroll *by Raphael Shaberman*
Sherlock Holmes and the author uncover new evidence in their investigations into the mysterious life and writing of Lewis Carroll. They examine published works by Carroll that have been overlooked by previous commentators. A newly-discovered poem, almost certainly by Carroll, is published here.
Amongst many aspects of Carroll's highly complex personality, this book explores his relationship with his parents, numerous child friends, and the formidable Mrs Liddell, mother of the immortal Alice. Raphael Shaberman was a founder member of the Lewis Carroll Society and a teacher of autistic children.
1994 • 118 pages • illustrated • ISBN 978-1-871551-13-6

Poetry in Exile: A study of the poetry of W.H. Auden, Joseph Brodsky & George Szirtes *by Michael Murphy*
"Michael Murphy discriminates the forms of exile and expatriation with the shrewdness of the cultural historian, the acuity of the literary critic, and the subtlety of a poet alert to the ways language and poetic form embody the precise contours of experience. His accounts of Auden, Brodsky and Szirtes not only cast much new light on the work of these complex and rewarding poets, but are themselves a pleasure to read." *Stan Smith, Research Professor in Literary Studies, Nottingham Trent University.*
Michael Murphy is a poet and critic. He teaches English literature at Liverpool Hope University College.
2004 • 266 pages • ISBN 978-1-871551-76-1

Wordsworth and Coleridge: Views from the Meticulous to the Sublime *by Andrew Keanie*
For a long time the received view of the collaborative relationship between Wordsworth and Coleridge has been that Wordsworth was the efficient producer of more finished poetic statements (most notably his long, autobiographical poem *The Prelude*) and Coleridge, however extraordinary he was as a thinker and a talker, left behind more intolerably diffuse and fragmented works. *Wordsworth and Coleridge: Views from the Meticulous to the Sublime* examines the issue from a number of different critical vantage points, reassessing the poets' inextricable achievements, and rediscovering their legacy.
Andrew Keanie is a lecturer at the University of Ulster. He is the author of articles on William Wordsworth, Samuel Taylor Coleridge and Hartley Coleridge. He has written three books for the Greenwich Exchange *Student Guide Literary Series* on Wordsworth, Coleridge and Byron.
2007 • 206 pages • ISBN 978-1-871551-87-7 (Hardback)

POETRY

Adam's Thoughts in Winter by *Warren Hope*
Warren Hope's poems have appeared from time to time in a number of literary periodicals, pamphlets and anthologies on both sides of the Atlantic. They appeal to lovers of poetry everywhere. His poems are brief, clear, frequently lyrical, characterised by wit, but often distinguished by tenderness. The poems gathered in this first book-length collection counter the brutalising ethos of contemporary life, speaking of, and for, the virtues of modesty, honesty and gentleness in an individual, memorable way.
2000 • 46 pages • ISBN 978-1-871551-40-2

Baudelaire: Les Fleurs du Mal *Translated by F.W. Leakey*
Selected poems from *Les Fleurs du Mal* are translated with parallel French texts and are designed to be read with pleasure by readers who have no French as well as those who are practised in the French language.
F.W. Leakey was Professor of French in the University of London. As a scholar, critic and teacher he specialised in the work of Baudelaire for 50 years and published a number of books on the poet.
2001 • 152 pages • ISBN 978-1-871551-10-5

'The Last Blackbird' and other poems by Ralph Hodgson *edited and introduced by John Harding*
Ralph Hodgson (1871-1962) was a poet and illustrator whose most influential and enduring work appeared to great acclaim just prior to, and during, the First World War. His work is imbued with a spiritual passion for the beauty of creation and the mystery of existence. This new selection brings together, for the first time in 40 years, some of the most beautiful and powerful 'hymns to life' in the English language.
John Harding lives in London. He is a freelance writer and teacher and is Ralph Hodgson's biographer.
2004 • 70 pages • ISBN 978-871551-81-5

Lines from the Stone Age by *Sean Haldane*
Reviewing Sean Haldane's 1992 volume *Desire in Belfast*, Robert Nye wrote in *The Times* that "Haldane can be sure of his place among the English poets." This place is not yet a conspicuous one, mainly because his early volumes appeared in Canada, and because he has earned his living by other means than literature. Despite this, his poems have always had their circle of readers. The 60 previously unpublished poems of *Lines from the Stone Age* – "lines of longing, terror, pride, lust and pain" – may widen this circle.
2000 • 52 pages • ISBN 978-1-871551-39-6

Lipstick *by Maggie Butt*
Lipstick is Maggie Butt's debut collection of poems and marks the entrance of a voice at once questioning and self-assured. She believes that poetry should be the tip of the stiletto which slips between the ribs directly into the heart. The poems of *Lipstick* are often deceptively simple, unafraid of focusing on such traditional themes as time, loss and love through a range of lenses and personae. Maggie Butt is capable of speaking in the voice of an 11th-century stonemason, a Himalayan villager, a 13-year-old anorexic. When writing of such everyday things as nylon sheets, jumble sales, X-rays or ginger beer, she brings to her subjects a dry humour and an acute insight. But beyond the intimate and domestic, her poems cover the world, from Mexico to Russia; they deal with war, with the resilience of women, and, most of all, with love.
Maggie Butt is head of Media and Communication at Middlesex University, London, where she has taught Creative Writing since 1990.
2007 • 72 pages • ISBN 978-1-871551-94-5

Martin Seymour-Smith – Collected Poems *edited by Peter Davies*
To the general public Martin Seymour-Smith (1928-1998) is known as a distinguished literary biographer, notably of Robert Graves, Rudyard Kipling and Thomas Hardy. To such figures as John Dover Wilson, William Empson, Stephen Spender and Anthony Burgess, he was regarded as one of the most independently-minded scholars of his generation, through his pioneering critical edition of Shakespeare's *Sonnets*, and his magisterial *Guide to Modern World Literature*.
To his fellow poets, Graves, James Reeves, C.H. Sisson and Robert Nye – he was first and foremost a poet. As this collection demonstrates, at the centre of the poems is a passionate engagement with Man, his sexuality and his personal relationships.
2006 • 182 pages • ISBN 978-1-871551-47-1

Shakespeare's Sonnets *by Martin Seymour-Smith*
Martin Seymour-Smith's outstanding achievement lies in the field of literary biography and criticism. In 1963 he produced his comprehensive edition, in the old spelling, of *Shakespeare's Sonnets* (here revised and corrected by himself and Peter Davies in 1998). With its landmark introduction and its brilliant critical commentary on each sonnet, it was praised by William Empson and John Dover Wilson. Stephen Spender said of him "I greatly admire Martin Seymour-Smith for the independence of his views and the great interest of his mind"; and both Robert Graves and Anthony Burgess described him as the leading critic of his time. His exegesis of the *Sonnets* remains unsurpassed.
2001 • 194 pages • ISBN 978-1-871551-38-9

The Rain and the Glass *by Robert Nye*
When Robert Nye's first poems were published, G.S. Fraser declared in the *Times Literary Supplement*: "Here is a proper poet, though it is hard to see how the larger literary public (greedy for flattery of their own concerns) could be brought to recognize that. But other proper poets – how many of them are left? – will recognize one of themselves."
Since then Nye has become known to a large public for his novels, especially *Falstaff* (1976), winner of the Hawthornden Prize and The Guardian Fiction Prize, and *The Late Mr Shakespeare* (1998). But his true vocation has always been poetry, and it is as a poet that he is best known to his fellow poets.
This book contains all the poems Nye has written since his *Collected Poems* of 1995, together with his own selection from that volume. An introduction, telling the story of his poetic beginnings, affirms Nye's unfashionable belief in inspiration, as well as defining that quality of unforced truth which distinguishes the best of his work: "I have spent my life trying to write poems, but the poems gathered here came mostly when I was not."
2005 • 132 pages • ISBN 978-1-871551-41-9

Wilderness *by Martin Seymour-Smith*
This is Martin Seymour-Smith's first publication of his poetry for more than twenty years. This collection of 36 poems is a fearless account of an inner life of love, frustration, guilt, laughter and the celebration of others. He is best known to the general public as the author of the controversial and bestselling *Hardy* (1994).
1994 • 52 pages • ISBN 978-1-871551-08-2

EDUCATION

Making School Work *by Andy Buck*
Full of practical examples, this book sets out a range of strategies for successful school leadership. It provides examples of tried and tested ideas to use when tackling some of the key challenges facing every school leader: This book aims to offer readers a range of practical approaches to both policy and leadership style, based around a series of case studies and school-based policies. Each chapter examines a key challenge facing school leaders and provides practical ideas and strategies that have been shown to work in schools.
A geography teacher since 1987, Andy Bucks' experience has included working as a head of department, head of year, deputy head and two headships, all in London schools.
2007 • 142 pages • ISBN 978-1-871551-52-5

Story: The Heart of the Matter *ed. Dr Maggie Butt*
What can't we get enough of? Food? Sex? Alcohol? Stories? We devour hundreds of stories every day in television news, magazines, novels, movies, jokes, plays, newspapers, and we never get tired of them. Stories always leave us hungry for more. In this book, 15 established writers explore their own practice and ideas about storymaking. These novelists, journalists, poets, screenwriters, playwrights, documentary makers, oral storytellers and stand-up comics are also leading academics in Creative Writing and Journalism in UK universities. What do they have in common? Story. Their examinations of storymaking shed new light on what different forms, media and genres have in common. These writers don't tell you how to write a play or novel or poem, but they offer personal insights which are the fruit of years of experience. They share some of the ways to create that all-important connection between the idea and the audience – how to make the magic happen.
2007 • 180 pages • ISBN 978-1-871551-93-8

HISTORICAL FACTION

The Secret Life of Elizabeth I *by Paul Doherty*
A detective story with a difference – tracking down the real Elizabeth I – capturing the atmosphere of Elizabethan and Jacobean England, with stunning results. Paul Doherty's original research shows Elizabeth I of England to be a strongwilled, brilliant ruler but also a woman with deep passions and fervent attachments. The lady-in-waiting describes the passionate relationship between Elizabeth and Robert Dudley, later Earl of Leicester. She reveals evidence about the strange death of Dudley's wife, the very physical relationship between Elizabeth and Dudley, and the stunning revelation that they had a son, Arthur Dudley, seized by the Spanish in 1587.
Paul Doherty is an internationally renowned author. He studied history at Liverpool and Oxford Universities, gaining his doctorate at Oxford. He is now the headmaster of a very successful London school. First in the series published by Greenwich Exchange.
2006 • 210 pages • ISBN 978-1-871551-85-3 (Hardback)

Death of the Red King *by Paul Doherty*
Was William Rufus, the Red King, accidentally killed by one of his own men while hunting or is there a more chilling interpretation of his death? Doherty demonstrates that the Red King's death is highly suspect. Walter Tirel has been cast as the villain of the piece. However, through the eyes of

Anselm the great philosopher, this faction develops a quite different version of his death.
Second in the series published by Greenwich Exchange.
2006 • 190 pages • ISBN 978-1-871551-92-1 (Hardback)

BUSINESS

English Language Skills *by Vera Hughes*
If you want to be sure, (as a student, or in your business or personal life), that your written English is correct, this book is for you. Vera Hughes' aim is to help you to remember the basic rules of spelling, grammar and punctuation. 'Noun', 'verb', 'subject', 'object' and 'adjective' are the only technical terms used. The book teaches the clear, accurate English required by the business and office world. It coaches acceptable current usage and makes the rules easier to remember.
Vera Hughes was a civil servant and is a trainer and author of training manuals.
2002 • 142 pages • ISBN 978-1-871551-60-0